147 Fun Things To Do In SALT LAKE CITY

written by
Karen Foulk

Into Fun Company Publications
A Division of Into Fun, Inc.
Sugar Land, Texas

147 Fun Things To Do In Salt Lake City
by Karen Foulk

Cover by Delton Gerdes
Map illustrations by Brockton Brown
Copyright © August 2002 Karen Foulk

Library of Congress Control Number: 2001099725

ISBN 0-9714736-1-7

Printed and bound in Canada

Into Fun Co. Publications are available for educational, business, and sales promotional use.

Into Fun, Inc.

P.O. Box 2494, Sugar Land, Texas 77487-2494
Phone: 281-980-9745   Fax: 281-494-9745
www.intofun.com

This book contains descriptions including operating times and admission costs of many of the fun and interesting places in the Salt Lake City area. Although a great deal of effort has gone into making this book as up-to-date and accurate as possible, changes constantly occur. Therefore, before visiting a destination, please call to confirm the information provided here. Neither Into Fun Co. Publications, a division of Into Fun, Inc., the owner, nor the author warrant the accuracy of the information in this book, which includes but is not limited to price changes, addresses, names, hours of operation, management or conditions of the attraction described.

When it comes to having fun—you're holding Salt Lake City in your hand. Let me show you 147 fun things to do right here, right now. You can entertain your guests, build family memories, impress a date, or dazzle your friends with all the fun places you know to go using this guide.

And I've made it easy, too. My book is so small it fits into the glove box of your car, your purse, or even your jacket pocket.

Salt Lake City abounds with Mormon sites. Take the complimentary tours—their history is incredible. The organ built by early Mormon settlers was a feat of pioneer engineering. Be sure to hear the Mormon Tabernacle Choir sing in the Tabernacle on Sunday mornings. Find out how desperately needed clothing, medical supplies, and food are flown within a few days to victims of natural disasters and war—all over the world. You'll find their humanitarian relief efforts so impressive, you'll want to get involved.

Most of all, visit the Family Search Center—there's nothing like it anywhere else. From their huge database of names, you can find all kinds of things about your family. And don't leave without eating at the Lion House; it's good food from old recipes handed down for generations. It's the Mormon cuisine.

What can I say briefly about Salt Lake City's outdoor recreation? Not enough. Just know you're only 25 minutes from some of the finest skiing ever. You don't have to make a lot of plans to go fly fishing; your fishing guide will pick you up at your hotel. If you can't wait, have your guide pick you up at the airport. And you're only a day's drive to some of the most scenic national parks imaginable. It's picture perfect for your camera.

I know you're having fun when I see you packing around my book and it's dog-eared. I'm tempted to give you mine, but it's dog-eared too. See you around. See you having fun.

Karen Foulk

With all my love,
to my husband, Don,
whom I have trouble
convincing that I am working.

To my wonderful children
who believe as I do — fun's important.
Michael & Amber,
Rachel & John,
David,
and
Rebecca.

Into Fun Company would like to thank the following individuals for their contributions in making this book a success.

Ken Barrow – for his legal advice

Brocky Brown – for his interest in N2 Fun's success

Kathy Buck – for her thorough and speedy editing efforts

Sharon Cooper – for her friendship— there are no better friends

Michael Foulk – for being Into Fun, Co.'s webmaster

Jerrie Hurd – for her interest and support

Merrill Littlewood – for his excellent insight and sound advise

TABLE OF CONTENTS

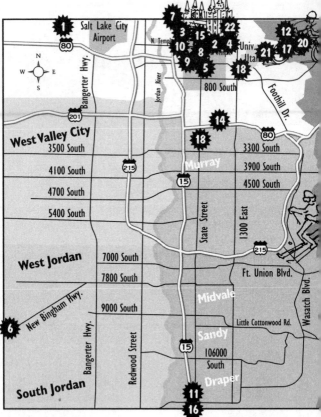

1. Antelope Island State Park
2. Beehive House
3. Family History Library
4. Family Search Center
5. Hansen Planetarium
6. Kennecott Copper Mine
7. Lagoon Amusement Park
8. Mormon Tabernacle Choir
9. Mormon Tabernacle Organ
10. Museum of Church History
11. North American Museum of Ancient Life

12. Old Deseret Village
13. Red Butte Gardens
14. Snelgrove Ice Cream Parlors
15. Temple Square
16. Thanksgiving Point
17. This Is The Place Heritage Park
18. Trax (Light Rail)
19. Trolley Square
20. Utah's Hogle Zoo
21. Utah's Museum of Fine Arts
22. Utah State Capitol

Salt Lake City Area

Carolea Andenberg

Chapter 1

WHAT'S SALT LAKE CITY GOT TO SHOW OFF?

ANTELOPE ISLAND STATE PARK

4528 West 1700 South, Sycacuse 84075
801-773-2941 801 322-3770 Camping

Salt Lake City's dead sea

Nothing else like it on earth! A desert island surrounded by a dead sea. Drive the 8-mile scenic paved loop. At sunrise, the rays on the water and hills make a colorful sight. So bring the camera.

A haven for wildlife. Amazingly, you'll see a lot of buffalo—about 600 of them. They're not native to the island, but they're protected here. Every October, watch the buffalo roundup—the public's invited.

On the far end of the island, an early settler built his adobe ranch house, in 1848. Self-guided tours offered year-round and free park admission, 801-554-9253. From the house, leave on horseback across open country with a guide. (This trailride is so unique, it's won awards.) Or take a horse-drawn wagon ride. Call for reservations before going, 801-782-4946.

Twenty-five miles of hiking and biking trails, some rugged. You'll need to bring along food and water. Not even a vending machine out here, though a small restaurant operates in the summer. Bountiful Bicycle Center rents bikes during the summer, 801-295-6711.

Go floating in the lake—the island has beaches with changing rooms. Or, daily during the summer, take a 1-hour scenic cruise of the lake from the marina.

Summer Hours (Winter hours vary)
Daily .... 7 am - 10 pm
Ranch House
Daily .... 10 am - 4 pm
Cost
Per car $7
Directions
From I-15, take exit #335 in Layton. Go left (west) on Antelope Dr. across the 7-mile causeway.

BEEHIVE HOUSE

67 East South Temple
Salt Lake City
801-240-2672
www.lds.org

Mansion of Utah's 1st governor

A beehive sits atop Brigham Young's charming old home. It symbolizes his work ethic of industry. (Utah is the beehive state.)

His home, built in 1854, was his residence while he served as President of the LDS Church and Governor of the Utah Territory.

Take the delightful 30-minute tour and see this beautifully restored home and all its period furnishings. Hear stories about this fascinating man who established Salt Lake City and made Mormon history. Now a National Historic Landmark.

Ask them about hosting parties.

Hours

Tours every 10 minutes
Mon. - Sat. . . . . 9:30 am - 4:30 pm
Sunday . . . . 10 am - 1 pm

Cost

Free

Directions

At the corner of State Street and South Temple.

FAMILY HISTORY LIBRARY

35 North West Temple Street
Salt Lake City 84105
801-240-2331
www.familysearch.org

The world's largest genealogy library

Nothing compares to the LDS Church's extensive collection of genealogical resources. It's by far the world's leading source of family research.

Tours available throughout the day.

Hours

Monday . . . . .7:30 am - 5 pm
Tues. - Sat. . . . . 7:30 am - 10 pm

Cost

Free

Directions

Across from Temple Square.

FAMILY SEARCH CENTER

Joseph Smith Memorial Building
15 East South Temple Street
Salt Lake City
801-240-4085

Discover your roots instantly

Researching your roots can be time consuming. But at the Family Search Center, it's instant. Simply type in your name in a provided computer and immediately discover things about your ancestors.

The LDS Church invites you to explore their genealogical data bank; it comprises over a billion names. Over 150 computers and friendly help await your arrival. Who knows—maybe you have royal blood?

Hours

Mon. - Sat. . . . . 9 am - 9 pm

Cost

Free

Directions

Located on the 1st and 4th floors of the Joseph Smith Memorial Building.

HANSEN PLANETARIUM

15 S. State Street
Salt Lake City 84111
801-538-2104

Not your usual planetarium

What makes this planetarium exceptional? The star shows are so good, they're considered some of the best in the nation. Call for times. Watch for their annual Christmas show *Star of Bethlehem*.

Laser shows too on weekends.

And a visit wouldn't be complete without taking time to see the moon rock and other exhibits.

Parking available at ZCMI's parking garage on South Temple.

Hours

Planetarium

Mon. - Thurs.	9 am - 9 pm
Saturday	9:30 am - Midnight
Sunday	Noon - 5:30 pm

Cost

(Star Show)

Adults	$4.50
Children 4 - 12	$3.50
Seniors 62+	$3.50

Directions

Downtown, inside the old City Public Library building, on State Street, between the Belvedere Condominiums and the Alta Club.

KENNECOTT UTAH COPPER'S BINGHAM CANYON MINE

Copperton
801-252-3234

So big, you can see it from the space shuttle

You've seen this giant copper mine in pictures, now see it for yourself. The Visitor Center has an observation area that lets you look down into the mine. It's 1/2-mile deep and 2-1/2-miles wide.

More than 15 million tons of copper metal has been removed from this hole, making it the largest man-made excavation in the world. There's nothing else like it. Now a National Historic Landmark.

Watch the video on mining in Utah.

Hours

April - October

Daily .... 8 am - 8 pm

Cost

Per car $4

Directions

From I-15, exit 7200 S. and go west to 7800 S. Go south on 7800 S., then west to the Bingham Highway (Hwy. 48). Then follow the signs to the mine.

LAGOON AMUSEMENT PARK

375 Lagoon Drive
Farmington 84025
801-451-8000

Utah's beloved amusement park

One of only a few parks that is family owned and operated. Clean, well-run, and so uncommercialized.

A new ride every year makes it a mandatory visit when school's out. Their 100-year-old carousel has entertained families for generations.

Brags of having 5 roller coasters. Bring your swimsuit and towel: admission includes the Lagoon-A-Beach water park.

Park entertainment perform here all summer. Call for schedule. Arcades, shops, and plenty of concessions. Or there's a picnic area inside the park. Ask about season tickets. Parking $6.

Stay at their RV park and campground next to the park with a handy convenience store nearby.

Hours

June, July, August, weekends in September & October

Mon. - Thurs. . . . . .11 am - 11 pm
Fri. & Sat. . . . . .11 am - Midnight
Sunday . . . . .11 am - 10:30 pm

Cost

51 inches to 64 years $29.95
Age 4 to 50 inches $23.95
Children age 3 and under $15.50
Seniors $16.50

Directions

Seventeen miles north of Salt Lake City.
From I-15N., exit #325, Lagoon Dr.

MORMON TABERNACLE CHOIR

Temple Square
50 West North Temple
Salt Lake City 84150
801-240-3221

World-famous choir

Hear the choir in concert most Sunday mornings—for free. Be in your seat in the tabernacle by 9:15 am; their broadcast performance "The Spoken Word" begins at 9:30 am. Or listen as they rehearse in the tabernacle on Thursday nights from 8 pm - 9 pm. It's informal, come and go as you like.

This renowned choir began in 1847 with a small group of amateur singers gathering to sing at the site for Temple Square.

The 325-member, all-volunteer choir has traveled the U.S. and foreign countries. Most often their performances are sold out.

Hours

Music and the Spoken Word

Sunday .... 9:30 am

Rehearsals

Thursday .... 8 pm - 9:30 pm

Cost

Free

Directions

On Temple Square.

MORMON TABERNACLE ORGAN

Temple Square
50 West North Temple
Salt Lake City 84150
801-240-3221

A feat of pioneer engineering

Building a pipe organ on the frontier was no small accomplishment. Brigham Young asked Joseph Harris Ridges, a fellow pioneer, to build it because Ridges grew up working in an English organ factory.

Finding materials for such an instrument was no easy task. Suitable wood was brought from 300 miles away—in the Parowan and Pine Valley mountains.

A hand-pump bellows first powered the organ, then water was used. Today, it runs on electricity.

Hear the organ play at noon every day during the summer or as it accompanies the Mormon Tabernacle Choir's broadcast on Sunday mornings at 9:30 am. The organ has its own distinctive sound.

Hours

Organ recitals
(Memorial Day through Labor Day)

Mon. - Sat. .... Noon
Sunday .... 2 pm

Cost

Free

Directions

On Temple Square.

MUSEUM OF CHURCH HISTORY AND ART

45 North West Temple
Salt Lake City 84150
801-240-2299

Utah history is Mormon history

If you want to understand Mormon history, this museum is the place to go.

Of course you'll find treasured artifacts like the Mormon handcart, the 1830s edition of the Book of Mormon, and an authentic 1847 pioneer log cabin. But your museum experience will be truly memorable if you take the complimentary 1-hour tour.

The museum also has a prized collection of art on display. See the art exhibits on church history.

Park free across the street at 103 North Temple.

Hours

(Closed Easter, Thanksgivings, Christmas, and New Year's)

Mon. - Fri. . . . . 9 am - 9 pm
Sat. & Sun. . . . . 10 am - 7 pm

Cost

Free

Directions

Across the street from
Temple Square to the northwest.

NORTH AMERICAN MUSEUM OF ANCIENT LIFE

Thanksgiving Point
3003 North Thanksgiving Way
Lehi 84043
801-766-5000
www.thanksgivingpoint.com

Museum big on dinosaurs

Claims to have more dinosaur skeleton exhibits than any other museum in the world.

A first-class dinosaur museum, recently opening. Offers plenty of interesting hands-on exhibits and an IMAX theater with the latest features. Shows begin on the hour. Call for reservations.

Walk through a star tunnel. See a monster sea turtle. Dig in a dino quarry. Watch paleontologists at work. Great gift shop with lots of dinosaur items.

Hours
Museum
Summer (Memorial Day - Labor Day)

Mon. - Sat.	10 am - 8 pm

Regular hours

Mon., Fri., Sat.	Noon - 8 pm
Tues. & Thurs.	Noon - 6 pm

Mammoth Screen

Mon. - Sat.	11 am - 8 pm

Cost
Museum

Adults	$3
Children 3 - 12	$3

Mammoth Screen

Adults	$7
Children 3 - 12	$5

Directions

Take I-15 south of downtown Salt Lake City. Exit 287. Go west to Thanksgiving Way. Turn left.

OLD DESERET VILLAGE

This Is The Place Heritage Park
2601 East Sunnyside Avenue
Salt Lake City 84108
801-582-1847

Salt Lake City's living museum

Walk the streets as they used to be. A re-created pioneer village with old historic buildings that have been painstakingly restored.

See women dressed in bonnets and long skirts, men at work in blacksmith shops. Let them tell about Utah's history. Ride in the horse-drawn wagon.

You'll see places like the old Cedar City Tithing Office, the Deseret Telegraph Office, and the Snelgrove Bootmaking Shop.

Special events like Pioneer Day or the Candlelight Christmas celebration are worth attending.

Ask about having a pioneer birthday party.

Hours

Memorial Day - Labor Day

Mon. - Sat. .... 10 am - 5 pm

Cost

Adults $6
Children 3 - 11 .... $4
Seniors $4
Family Pass $20

Directions

At the mouth of Emigration Canyon, across from Hogle Zoo. Take 800 South east toward the mountains. The street will become Sunnyside Ave.

RED BUTTE GARDEN

300 Wakara Way (2250 East)
Salt Lake City 84108
801-581-4747
www.redbutte.utah.edu

A reclaimed garbage heap

Over 150 acres of lovely manicured gardens and nature areas with groomed trails only minutes from downtown. Open year-round.

Hike with a naturalist on Mondays or on the 2nd Saturday of every month. Hikes start from the visitor center. New children's garden. Gift shop.

Plenty of events make going often a must. Award-winning concerts perform in the garden's amphitheate during the summer`. Purchase tickets online. Offers children's programs and birthday parties. Part of the University of Utah.

Hours

May - September

Mon. - Sat.	9 am - 8 pm
Sunday	9 am - 5 pm

October - April

Tues. - Sun.	10 am - 5 pm

Cost

Adults	$5
Children 4 - 17	$3
Seniors 60+	$3

Directions

From I-15, exit 600 S. and go east to 1300 E. Turn left and travel 1 block north to 500 S., then turn right and head east.

SNELGROVE ICE CREAM PARLOR

850 East 2100 South
Salt Lake City 84106
801-485-8932

Salt Lake City's homegrown ice cream parlors

Utah's tastiest ice cream. Order their double thick milk shakes (any flavor) or their Create-Your-Own Splits (any flavor).

Local favorites include the Cashew Conquistador and the Fiesta Fruit—a lemon-lime soda fruit slush. But the all-time, best-selling ice cream flavors are Almond Fudge and Caramel Cashew.

During the holiday season, there's always a rush for their Peppermint Ice Cream.

Lots of flavors. They have what you like.

Hours

Mon. - Thurs.	11 am - 10 pm
Fri. & Sat.	11 am - 11 pm

Cost

Single	$1.85
Double	$2.85
Single waffle	$2.30

Other Locations:

605 East 400 South
801-359-4207

and

1005 East Fort Union (7200 South)
801-566-4322

Directions

From I-15 S., exit I-80 E. towards Cheyenne. Then exit 7th E. Turn left. Then right on 2100 S. Watch for the giant twirling ice cream cone.

TEMPLE SQUARE

50 West North Temple
Salt Lake City 84150
801-240-4872
www.lds.org

Mormon Church's ultimate site

Brigham Young designated this site for a temple only 4 days after he entered the Salt Lake Valley. He placed the cornerstone here in 1853, but it took over 40 years to actually build the temple.

Get the most from your visit: Take the complimentary tours at the different sites. See the historic tabernacle, the Assembly Hall, the visitor centers. Walk the gorgeous landscaped grounds.

Gain a better understanding of the LDS Church— commonly referred to as the Mormons. Now the fastest-growing church in America.

Spectacular during the holidays, with thousands of decorative lights and nativity scenes. Hear the Mormon Tabernacle Choir sing carols in their annaul Christmas performance *The Joy of Christmas* held on 2 nights in December in the new Conference Center.

Hours
Daily .... 9 am - 9 pm
Cost
Free
Directions
Center of downtown Salt Lake City.

THANKSGIVING POINT INSTITUTE

3003 N. Thanksgiving Way
Lehi 84043
801-768-2300
www.thanksgiving.com

A rich man's dream of giving thanks

Alan Ashton, a wealthy business man, dreamed of giving something back to his community. He loved learning and wanted to emphasize education. So he create Thanksgiving Point from a one-time dairy farm.

The institute includes an 18-hole championship golf course. Utah's Golf Hall of Fame is in the clubhouse. Visit the lovely Thanksgiving Garden, the Children's Discovery Garden, and the Country Farm Animal Park. The complex includes the Museum of Ancient Life with its large collection of dinosaur skeletons and the Mammoth Screen IMAX Theater. Browse through the Village shops featuring an old-fashioned soda fountain and more.

Hours

Thanksgiving & Children's Discovery Gardens
Mon. - Fri. . . . . 10 am - 9 pm
Saturday . . . . 9 am - 9 pm

Farm Country Animal Park
Mon. - Sat. . . . . 9 am - 9 pm

Museum of Ancient Life
Mon. - Sat. . . . . 10 am - 8 pm

Mammoth Screen Theater
Mon. - Sat. . . . . 11 am - 8 pm

Cost

Prices vary for each venue. Ask about the Discovery Passport that includes all 5 venues.

Directions

From Salt Lake City. Take I-15 S. and exit #287.

THIS IS THE PLACE HERITAGE PARK

2601 E. Sunnyside Avenue (800 South)
Salt Lake City 84108
801-582-1847
www.thisistheplace.org

Look out over the valley as Brigham Young did

Here's the monument dedicated to Brigham Young and his pioneer followers when they entered the Great Salt Lake Valley.

But it was 17 miles above this site—at Big Mountain Pass—where Young rose from his wagon's sick bed and said, "It is enough. This is the *right* place. Drive on." This began the great Mormon migration. Pioneers walked across the plains, pulling their handcarts to get here.

Brigham Young is known as a great western colonizer who faced enormous odds to establishing a settlement here.

View the valley. Browse through the visitor center and gift shop. Visit Old Deseret Village, a re-created pioneer village that's open Memorial Day through Labor Day weekend. The park is open year-round.

Across from Hogle Zoo.

Hours

Daily . . . . Dawn - Dusk

Cost

Free

Directions

At the mouth of Emigration Canyon, across from Hogle Zoo. Take 800 South east towards the mountains. The street will become Sunnyside Ave.

TRAX

Utah Transit Authority
Transit Express (TRAX)
Salt Lake City
801-743-3882
www.rideuta.com

Breeze through Salt Lake City

Salt Lake City loves its new light rail.

Trains operate daily from 10000 South (in Sandy) to the Delta Center (downtown), and the trip takes only 35 minutes. The 15-mile line stretch has 16 stations and 11 free Park & Ride lots.

The other 2.5-mile line runs from the Delta Center to the University's Rice Eccles Stadium, with 4 stations. The 2 lines connect at Main Street.

Trains stop every 10 minutes during peak hours and every 15 minutes at off-peak hours. On Sundays the wait is longer.

Tickets cost $1 for 2 hours or $2 for the day. But the downtown area is free. Schedules for the trains are online. Purchase tickets at station vending machines.

Hours

(No service New Year's Day, Thanksgiving & Christmas)

Mon. - Sat. .... 5 am - 11:20 pm
Sunday .... 10 am - 7 pm

Cost

For 2 hours $1
All day $2
Downtown area .... Free

TROLLEY SQUARE

600 South 700 East
Salt Lake City 84102
801-521-9877

Shop the old trolley barns

Shop historic Trolley Square. Over 70 shops in what were Salt Lake City's old trolley barns. Lots of specialty shops including an old-fashioned taffy store. You'll also find the U.S. Olympic Spirit Store for souvenirs. Art galleries, jewelers, apparel stores, and more. Also a place for children to play while parents shop.

Families enjoy favorites like the Hard Rock Cafe and the Old Spaghetti Factory. The Pub's Desert Edge Brewery allows children until 6 pm, and the food is tasty.

Watch a comedy show at Trolley Square Live, family oriented, 801-363-4474.

Hours

Mon. - Sat. .... 10 am - 9 pm
Sunday .... Noon - 5 pm

Directions

Take 600 South to 700 east.

UTAH'S HOGLE ZOO

2600 E. Sunnyside Avenue (800 South)
Salt Lake City 84108
801-582-1631
www.hoglezoo.org

Old zoo's looking good for the Olympics

All spruced up for the 2002 Olympics with a new $5.8 million entry. See hundreds of animals from around the world, many native to Utah. Ride the miniature train that's operated in the park over 30 years. New food area. Gift shop. Memberships allow admission into many other zoos.

The zoo opened in 1931. It's located at the mouth of Emigration Canyon, across from This Is The Place Heritage Park and Old Deseret Village.

Hours

(Closed Christmas & New Year's Day)
Summer

Daily (Zoo) .... 9 am - 5 pm
Daily (The Grounds) .....9 am - 6:30 pm
Winter
Daily (Zoo) .... 9 am - 4 pm
Daily (The Grounds) .... 9 am - 5 pm

Cost

Adults $7
Children 3 - 12 .... $5
Seniors 65+ $5

Directions

Take 800 South east toward the mountains. The street will become Sunnyside Avenue.

UTAH MUSEUM OF FINE ART

University of Utah
410 Central Campus Drive
Salt Lake City 84112
801-581-7332
www.utah.edu/umfa

Utah's only fine art museum

Visit Utah's finest fine art museum in its new 74,000 square foot, award-winning building. It features 20 galleries, a cafe with outdoor dining (weather permitting) a nifty museum store, and an outdoor sculpture garden. Located on the University of Utah campus. Plenty of visitor parking.

Tours are self guided so take your time seeing the collection. Highlights include the new galleries featuring Utah art, contemporary art, decorative arts, and art of the West. See the Ethnic Man.

Offers educational programs like Kidmuse art activities for families.

Hours

Mon. - Fri. . . . . 10 am - 5 pm
Sat. & Sun. . . . . Noon - 5 pm

Cost

Free

Directions

On the University of Utah campus. From downtown take 400 South east to the University of Utah's Campus Center Dr.

UTAH STATE CAPITOL

350 North Main Street
Salt Lake City 84114
801-538-3000
801-538-1563 Tours

See this historic landmark

and the gravitational mystery spot behind it

Pick up a brochure and take a self-guided tour of the capitol building. Guided tours take place every half hour. Meet at the huge relief map on the 1st floor.

Highlights include the 165-foot rotunda painted with seagulls that are bigger than they appear–some have wing span of 6 feet. From this massive dome hangs a 95-foot, 7000-pound chain that supports a 6000-pound chandelier.

Don't miss seeing the race car that broke speed records on the Bonneville Salt Flats.

A few blocks north of the Capitol, take the little road down the canyon. Watch for a 2nd road that veers uphill. Stay on the main road another 100 feet down the hill. Stop and put your car in neutral. The car will coast *uphill* out of the canyon. This is Salt Lake City's mystery spot, "Gravity Hill"–an optical illusion.

Hours
Capitol
Mon. - Fri. (June, July, August) . 6 am - 8 pm
Mon. - Fri. (Sept. - May) . . . . . . 6 am - 6 pm
Guided Tours every half hour
Mon. - Fri. . . . . 9 am - 4 pm
Cost
Free
Directions
The north end of State St., north of Temple Square.

29

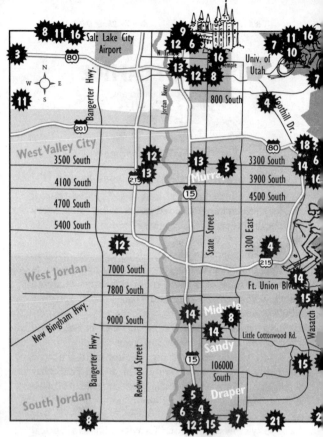

1. Alta Ski Area
2. Brighton Ski Area
3. Bonneville Salt Flats
4. Fly Fishing
5. Float Trips
6. Golf Courses
7. Hiking Trails
8. Horseback Riding
9. Lava Hot Springs
10. Mormon Pioneer Trail
11. Mountain Biking
12. Olympic Village & Venues
13. Professional Sports Teams
14. Rock Climbing
15. Scenic Drives
16. Sleigh Rides and Wagon Rides
17. Snowbird Ski & Summer Resort
18. Snowmobiling
19. Solitude Ski Resort
20. Sundance Ski Resort
21. Timanogos Cave National Monument

Salt Lake City Area

Chapter 2
OUT IN NATURE, SPORTS , & SKI RESORTS

ALTA SKI AREA

P.O. Box 8007, Alta 84092
801-359-1078 Office
801-572-3939 Snow Report
www.alta.com

Ski as high as 10,550 feet

Fabulous powder snow and ski trails for all levels of skier. Having an average snow base of 500 inches. Helicopter and backcountry tours.

Offers lodging, including furnished condos. Plenty of dining. Season passes available.

Having a ski ticket good for both Alta and Snowbird Resorts that includes 4700 acres of skiing with 18 chair lifts. No snowboarding allowed. Family friendly.

Lift Hours

Opening the weekend before Thanksgiving, weather permitting

Daily . . . . 9:15 am - 4:30 pm
Half day . . . . 9:15 am - 1 pm & 1 pm - 4:30 pm

Cost

Individual tickets

Full day, all lifts $38
Half day, all lifts $29
Full day, beginner lifts $22
Single ride, any lift $5
4 single tows . . . . Free

Directions

Take I-15 S. to I-215 E. Exit #6, 6200 S., and go right on Wasatch Blvd. Follow the signs to Little Cottonwood Canyon.

BRIGHTON SKI AREA

Big Cottonwood Canyon
Star Route, Brighton 84121
801-532-4731   800-873-5512
www.skibrighton.com

One of the nations's top ten ski resorts

A world-class ski resort where locals love to ski as well as outsiders because of its great value and excellent snow conditions. Children under 10 ski free. Snowboarders welcome.

One of the oldest resorts, but also one of the most modern, having 3 high-speed chair lifts. Ski 66 runs down 2 mountains.

Ski rentals, plenty of dining, and lodging available. Season passes. Buy ski tickets good for both Brighton and Solitude resorts, that have a connecting ski run. Only 45 minutes from downtown.

Lift Hours

Daily (Regular)	9 am - 4 pm
Half day . . . . . 9 am - 12:30 pm & 12:30 pm - 4	
Mon. - Sat. (Twilight)	4 pm - 9 pm
Mon. - Sat. (Super Day)	9 am - 9 pm

Cost

Adult Day Pass	$39
Adult Half Day	$34
Adult Super Day	$45
Seniors 70+	$10
Children 10 and under	Free
5-pack coupons	$160
Solbright ticket (2 ski resorts)	$59

Directions

From downtown, take 700 E. to I-80 E. Follow to I-215 S. Take I-215 S. and exit 6200 S. Stay left (it will turn into Wasatch Blvd.), then left up canyon.

BONNEVILLE SALT FLATS

Bureau of Land Management
801-977-4300

So flat you can see the earth's curvature.

Bonneville Salt Flats—very desolate. It's 30,000 acres with a fragile eco system that's void of any life. Made up of sodium chloride—table salt; One of Utah's most unique natural features. Designated an Area of Critical Environmental Concern.

The salt flats formed after ancient Lake Bonneville evaporated. The Great Salt Lake is all that's left of this huge lake. In the winter, a shallow layer of water covers the surface. Then in the spring, the water slowly evaporates; the winds create a nearly perfect plain.

National speed records have been set here by world-class drivers. In 1914, race driver Teddy Tetzieff drove what was then an unbelievable speed of 141.73 m.p.h. In 1970, Gary Gabelich set records in his rocket powered car Blue Fame at 622.407 m.p.h. Speed Week is always held at the end of August.

Jim Bridger explored the Great Salt Lake Desert in 1824. Captain B.L.E. Bonneville sent an expedition here in 1833. Although the salt flats bear his named, but he never saw them. The salt flats also contribute to the Donner-Reed Party's tragedy in Sierra Nevada. The party ended up leaving needed supplies behind when their wagons got stuck in the salty mud.

At all times, keep your vehicle on the road. What you're looking at may be only a thin crust of salt with gooey mud underneath. Be prepared for desert conditions, no services accept during racing season. Accommodations Wendover, 10 miles to the west.

Directions
Take I-80 W. about 80 miles and take exit #4.
Drive north a few miles.

FLY FISHING

Four Seasons Flyfishers
6591 South 1460 West
Murray 84123, 801-288-1028

Fly fish with a outfitter with 12 years of experience on local waters. Beginners welcome, will include equipment. Half-days and full-day trips.

Provo River Outfitters Flyfishing

Guide Service
916 East 1150 North
Pleasant Grove 84062
801-785-5260   888-PRO-UTAH
www.utahflyfishing.com

Only 45 minutes from Salt Lake City, offers the Provo River–tops for flyfishing. Offers 4-, 6-, and 8-hour guided trips for brown, rainbow trout, and cutthroat. Beginners welcome. Equipment, flie, and instructions included. Lunches provided on full-day trips. Transportation can be arranged. Open year-round. Call to make reservations.

Western Rivers Flyfisher
1071 East 900 South
Salt Lake City 84105
801-521-6424   800-545-4312
www.wrflyfisher.com

Guided flyfishermen since 1986; fishing trips on Provo, Green Rivers, and other places. Well-known for their excellent service, teaches fly tying and beginning fishing. Day trips with lunch. Will pick up at your hotel. Extra for equipment. Call to make reservations.

FLOAT TRIPS

HIGH COUNTRY RAFTING

512 East 4750 North, Provo 84604
801-224-2500 www.highcountryrafting.com.

Offering 2-hour trips down the Provo River, between Mt. Timpanogos and Cascade Peak in Provo Canyon. May - October. Families welcome.

HOLIDAY EXPEDITIONS

544 East 3900 South, Salt Lake City 84107
801-266-2087 800-624-6323
www.bikeraft.com

For a rafting vacation on the Colorado, Green, and Salmon Rivers. Also trips in the Dinosaur and Canyonland National Parks and Baja Mexico. Some trips have age limits. May - October.

MOKI MAC RIVER EXPEDITIONS

P.O. Box 71242, Salt Lake City 84171
801-268-6667 www.mokimac.com

Rafting vacations on the Green and Colorado Rivers. River rafting trips from 1-14 days. Canoe rentals for the Green River. April - October.

PARK CITY RAFTING

1105 N. Taggart Lane, Morgan 84050
435-655-3800

Rafting trips for families ages 4 and older. Take a 2-hour whitewater trip on class II-III rapids down the Weber River near Park City. May - early September.

WESTERN RIVER EXPEDITIONS

800-453-7450 801-942-6669 www.westernriver.com

Offers a variety of rafting trips down the Colorado, Green, and Salmon Rivers with everything you need, including gourmet meals cooked outdoors.

18-HOLE GOLF COURSES

BONNEVILLE GOLF COURSE

954 Conner Street, Salt Lake City 801-583-9513
One of the Salt Lake City area's oldest but finest. Challenging, hilly, and picturesque with shots over ravines and creeks. Tee times: 801-484-3333.

MOUNTAIN DELL GOLF COURSE

Parley's Canyon, Salt Lake City 801-582-3812
On the way to Park City, a mountain course in beautiful canyon overlooking a reservoir. Beware of the wildlife. Tee time: 801-484-3333.

PARK MEADOW GOLF CLUB

2000 Meadow Drive, Park City 801-531-7029
Another of the city's best 18-hole courses, designed by Jack Nicklaus, in the Scottish link tradition. Great clubhouse and practice range, 801-531-7029.

RIVERBEND GOLF COURSE

12800 South 1040 West, Salt Lake City 801-253-3673
A great course. Play 9 holes atop a bluff, 9 holes below along the river. Tee time: 801-253-3673.

THANKSGIVING POINT GOLF COURSE

2095 North West Frontage Road, Lehi 801-768-7400
New. One of the finest in the West, designed by Johnny Miller. Hosts Utah Open, 801-768-7400.

THE HOMESTEAD

700 N. Homestead Drive, Midway 801-654-1102
A very fine course with breathtaking mountain views. Popular with vacationers, 801-654-1102.

WASATCH MOUNTAIN STATE PARK

N. Homestead Drive, Midway 435-654-0532
In a state park, with a 4-star rating by Golf Digest. Stunning views, 801-266-0268.

HIKING TRAILS

BONNEVILLE SHORELINE TRAIL

P.O. Box 581136 Salt Lake City 84158 801-816-0876

Not all of the 90-mile trail is ready for hiking and biking. But when it is, it will run across the foothills of the Wasatch Front along what was the eastern shoreline of ancient Lake Bonneville—from Brigham City to Nephi. A section of the trail is complete from Emigration Canyon to City Creek. Trailhead at This is the Place Heritage Park.

MOUNT TIMPANOGOS PERIMETER TRAIL

Pleasant Grove Ranger District
435-785-3563

An 18-mile trail rising nearly 6000 feet in elevation in the Uinta National Forest. One of the most scenic hikes in the area. Climb past a number of waterfalls and meadow to the 11,750-foot peak. Below the summit, lies Emerald Lake. From State Route 92, a trailhead is just past the Sundance Resort at Theater in the Pines. Another one is over the ridge in American Fork Canyon at Timpooneke. Both trails are 9 miles long and for experienced hikers only and it can be done in a day. The view from on top is unbelievably stunning.

WASATCH CREST TRAIL

A popular hike for experienced hikers. Twenty-two miles of scenic hiking that begins at Big Water Trail at the end Mill Creek Canyon. A part of the Great Western Trail that runs from Canada to Mexico. Pay a fee at the station located at the mouth of Mill Canyon.

HORSEBACK RIDING

FIELDING GARR RANCH HOUSE

R & G Horse & Wagon Company
Antelope Island State Park, 801-782-4946

Voted # 2, the Best of Road Award for being a unique attraction, offers guided horseback riding in open backcountry; see the buffalo. By reservation.

CARRIAGE FOR HIRE

428 West 200 North, Salt Lake City 84103, 801-363-8687

Guided 1-hour horseback riding along the beautiful Bonneville Shoreline Trail from This Is The Place Heritage Park, $25/hour.

HOMESTEAD HORSEBACK RIDING

975 West Golf Course Drive, Midway 84049
435-654-5810   888-472-7669

Guided trail rides in Wasatch Mountain State Park, where the movie *Jeremiah Jones* was filmed, starring Robert Redford. Barnyard rides for kids age 8 and younger. 1-hour $30; Picnic ride $55.

OUTLAW COUNTRY ADVENTURES

6965 Union Park Center #400, Midvale 84047
801-304-0042   www.outlawcountryadventures.com

Your horseback riding adventure is custom made to your liking—no experience necessary. Scenic day rides, backcountry rides anywhere in Utah. Will provide camping equipment and meals. By reservation.

SUNRISE STABLES

3059 West 14750 South, Riverton 84065   801-254-1081

Only 30 minutes from Salt Lake City, rent horses to ride along the Jordan River Parkway, $20/hour. Guides cost an extra $20, if you want one. Open daily at 10 am until dusk.

LAVA HOT SPRINGS WORLD FAMOUS HOT BATHS & OLYMPIC SWIMMING COMPLEX

430 East Main Street, Lava Hot Springs, Idaho 83246
208-776-5221   800-423-8597   www.lavahotsprings.com

Even the Indians came here to relax

Only 2 hours from Salt Lake City, soak in hot pools filled with bubbling natural underground spring mineral water—no sulfur smells. Open year round. The spring's temperature ranges from 102-114 degrees, depending on where you're standing in the pool. On cold winter nights, the steam creates a cloud over the pools, making it all the more private.

In the summer, the complex opens their swimming pools, including an Olympic-sized pool. Tube slides and a 33-foot diving tower. Take the family.

In the past, these waters were thought to have healing abilities, and this area was a popular gathering place—even for the Indians.

Hours

April - September

Daily. . . . . 8 am - 11 pm

October - March

Daily . . . . 9 am - 10 pm

Cost

Adults $4.50
Children 4 - 11 . . . . $4
Children age 3 & under . . . . Free
Mon. - Thurs. (Family Pass) $11

Directions

Take I-15 N. towards Pocatello, ID. About 20 miles before Pocatello, exit #47 McCammon. Go east on Hwy. 3 for 11 miles.

MORMON PIONEER TRAIL

Utah State Parks and Recreation

The Donner Party, the Pony Express and the Mormon Pioneers used this trail

Follow the footsteps of the Mormon pioneers as they made their way from East Canyon up to Big Mountain Pass. Atop Big Mountain Pass, Brigham Young rose from his wagon sick bed and said, "It is enough. This is the *right* place. Drive on." Relive this great historic moment as you gaze out across the Salt Lake Valley, just as he did.

The trail is 4.6 miles long with a vertical rise of 1400 feet, to an altitude of 7400 feet at the pass. It begins at the pioneer camp site at East Canyon Road. You'll cross the East Canyon Creek footbridge and follow a path the winds alongside a creek. The trail climbs up Little Emigration Canyon.

The trail ends at Highway U-65 at the ridge line. A historical marker marks the spot. From the marker, the Great Western Trail heads south if you want to extend your journey.

Finding places to follow on the Mormon Pioneer Trail is difficult. This section of the trail, but, is open to the public and is maintained by the Utah State Parks and Recreation. The trail's is at its best mid-June through October or before the snow returns.

Directions

From Salt Lake City, take I-80 E. to Parley's Summit. Just after the summit, exit Jeremy Ranch and go north under the freeway. Turn left at the stop sign and right on Jeremy Ranch Dr. Continue until the road turns sharply to the right. Look for East Canyon Rd.–a dirt road on the left. Drive 4.9 miles to the parking lot for the trail on the left.

MOUNTAIN BIKING

ANTELOPE ISLAND STATE PARK

4528 West 1700 South, Sycacuse 84075
801-773-2941 Visitor Center

Over 25 miles of biking trails including rugged mountain terrain. Biking along the 9-mile White Rock Loop is an excellent way into the diverse ecology and geology of the island. The 7.2-mile causeway to the island has a bike lane too. The following bicycle shops rent bikes: Bountiful Bicycles, 801-295-6711, and Wasatch Touring, 801-339-9361.

BIG & LITTLE COTTONWOOD CANYONS

Bikers love the steep 30-mile windy climb up the Big Cottonwood Canyon, or better yet, the exhilarating downhill thrill. Little Cottonwood Canyon is a favorite high altitude training ride.

BONNEVILLE SHORELINE TRAIL

P.O. Box 581136 Salt Lake City 84158   801-816-0876

Not all of the 90-mile trail is ready for hiking and biking. But when it is, it will run across the foothills of the Wasatch Range along what was once the eastern shoreline of ancient Lake Bonneville from Brigham City to Nephi. A section of the trail is complete from Emigration Canyon to City Creek. Find that trailhead at This is the Place Heritage Park.

COPPER PIT OVERLOOK

Tooele Chamber of Commerce and Tourism
800-378-0690

An uphill 19-mile ride to a view of the Kennecott Copper Mine, the largest man-made excavation. Begin at County Museum in Tooele, southwest of Salt Lake City. The trail takes you through Middle Canyon up West Mountain Summit to the overlook.

HOLIDAY EXPEDITIONS
544 East 3900 South, Salt Lake City 84107
801-266-2087   800-624-6323   www.bikeraft.com

Professional outfitter offers 3 trips in back country of the Colorado River Plateau, 2 in Canyonlands National Park, and in Dinosaur National Monument. Includes 35 years of experience, guides, meals, and bicycle rentals. Trips for athletic beginners to experts. $420-$876.

HOMESTEAD BIKING
975 West Golf Course Drive, Midway 84049
435-654-5810   888-472-7669

Ride the scenic trails at Wasatch Mountain State Park in Heber Valley. Offers rentals of: mountain bikes, road bikes, and child carriers. Helmets included.

One hour $6
Twelve hours $20

Nineteen-mile ride to the top of the Oquirrah Mountains. From on top, view the Kennecott Copper Mines, the world's largest man-made excavation.

MORMON TRAIL LOOP
800-378-0690

A 50-mile, year-round trail with stunning views of the Stansbury Mountains in Tooele County.

SACRED BEAR ADVENTURES
33 Racquet Club Drive, Park City 84068
435-655-7250   www.sacredbear.com

Quality half-day guided trips for novices that begin with a ride up one of the chair lifts in Park City, Deer Valley, and the Cottonwood Canyons, early June - September. Quality full-day guided rides for intermediates that explore a diversity of Wasatch and Unitas mountain trails, $75. All rides begin at the Cole Sports Store in Park City. Rentals available.

SKYLINE DRIVE

Only passable during summer months, considered the "highway to heaven." Rough, unpaved road atop the Wasatch Plateau. Fifty miles long, above 10,000 feet, the view is stunning–Alpine forest surrounded by desert land. Access the trail from the following cities: Mt. Pleasant, Ephraim, Spring City, and Manti. Part of the Great Western Trail.

SOLITUDE MOUNTAIN RESORT

12000 Big Cottonwood Canyon, Solitude 84121
801-534-1400   800-748-4754   www.skisolitude.com

A summer resort too. Chair lift takes bikers on a scenic ride to biking trails. Solitude Canyon offers over 20 miles of trails. Rent bikes at the Stone Haus.

SNOWBIRD SKI AND SUMMER RESORT

Little Cottonwood Canyon, Snowbird 84012
801-742-2222   www.snowbird.com

Take the tram to the top of the mountain for a spectacular thrilling bike ride downhill from 11,000 feet. July through September, weather permitting. Rentals available. In August, the annual 12-mile Hill Climb goes from Sandy to the resort.

STANSBURY FRONT TRAIL

Considered Tooele's ultimate mountain-biking trail. Twenty-five miles of the Stanbury Mountain grandeur. Desolate countryside in Tooele County away from all services. Go prepared with all necessities.

WASATCH CREST TRAIL

A popular biking trail–22 miles long beginning at the end of Mill Creek Canyon on Big Water Trail. A part of the Great Western Trail–Canada to Mexico. Bikes on trails only on even calendar days. A fee is charged for driving up Mill Creek Canyon.

OLYMPIC VILLAGE & VENUES

DEER VALLEY RESORT
Park City , 435-649-1000
Venue for:
Slalom, Combined Slalom, Freestyle Aerials &
Freestyle Moguls
(In the summer, ride scenic lift. Hike or bike
down the several 5-mile trails.)

ICE SHEET AT OGDEN
Weber State University, 4390 Harrison Boulevard
Ogden, 801-399-8750
Venue for:
Curling
(Try curling or ice hockey, public skating)

E CENTER
3200 South Decker Lake Drive
West Valley City 801-988-8000
Venue for:
Ice Hockey & Paralympic Ice Sledge Hockey
(Home of Utah Grizzlies & Utah Freezz teams.)

PARK CITY MOUNTAIN RESORT
Park City 435-649-8111
Venue for:
Giant Slalom & Snowboarding
(Ice skating, sleigh riding, tubing, snowshoeing &
skiing in winter; the Alpine slide, hiking, mountain
biking, horseriding, and hot-air ballooning in summer.)

PEAKS ICE ARENA
100 North Seven Peaks Boulevard, Provo, 801-377-8777
Venue for:
Ice Hockey
(Open for public skating, hockey & indoor soccer.)

SALT LAKE CITY ICE CENTER (DELTA CENTER)

301 West South Temple, Salt Lake City, 801-325-2013
Venue for:
Figure Skating & Short Track Speed Skating
(Downtown Salt Lake. Home of Utah Jazz,
concerts, rodeos, and ice shows.)

SOLDIER HOLLOW

Wasatch Mountain State Park, 435-654-1791
Venue for:
Biathlon, Cross-Country Skiing, Nordic
Combined, Paralympic Biathlon, and Paralympic
Cross-Country Skiing
(Near Heber City. Activities at Homestead
Resort & on the Heber Valley Historic Railroad.)

SNOWBASIN SKI AREA

Star Route 226, Ogden, 801-399-0304
Venue for:
Downhill, Combined Downhill, Super-G &
All Paralympic Alpine Skiing
(Hiking & biking in summer. Skiing in winter.)

UTAH OLYMPIC OVAL

5662 South 4800 West Kearns, 801-966-4229
Venue for:
Speed Skating
(Open for public skating.)

UTAH OLYMPIC PARK

Park City, 435-658-4200
Venue for:
Bobsleigh, Luge, Skeleton, Ski
Jumping, & Nordic Combined
(Guided tours of the park. Try ski jumping on one
of the smaller hills, or bobsled down the course
with a professional driver.)

PROFESSIONAL SPORTS TEAMS

Utah Blitzz

123 North Wright Brothers Drive, Suite 100
Salt Lake City 84116
801-401-8000 Box office   www.utahblitz.com

In 2001, the Blitzz—Salt Lake City's professional soccer team—won the United Soccer Leagues D3 National Championship at Franklin-Covey Field. Their season runs April - August. Purchase tickets through their box office or from Smith Tix, 801-467-TIXX.

Utah Grizzlies

E-Center
3200 South Decker Lake Drive
Salt Lake City 84119
801-988-8000   www.utahgrizz.com

Utah's minor league hockey team, member of the American Hockey League, an affiliate with the Dallas Stars. Season runs October through April. For tickets call 810-988-PUCK.

Utah Jazz

Delta Center
301 West South Temple
Salt Lake City 84101
801-325-2500

Utah's NBA basketball team. Season, October through April. Season tickets, 801-325-2548; Individual tickets, 801-325-SEAT.

Utah Starzz

Delta Center
301 West South Temple
Salt Lake City 84101
801-325-STAR   www.utahstarzz.com

Women's National Basketball Association (WNBA). Season, May - August. 801-325-STAR.

ROCK CLIMBING

Extreme Sports Center

8700 South Sandy Parkway
Sandy 84070
801-562-1400

Learn to rock climb on this center's 3-story rock climbing wall. Open to beginners as well as experts. Different climbing routes to the top. Some very difficult, others easy. Sign up for instructions.

Exum Mountain Adventures

7350 S. Wasatch Boulevard (3000 S.)
Salt Lake City
801-272-7338

This company teaches rock climbing in the great outdoors with professionally licensed instructors. Climb in Big and Little Cottonwood Canyons.

Rockreation Sport Climbing

2074 East 3900 South
Salt Lake City
801-278-7473

Rock climbing classes for beginners, intermediates, and experts. Learn to belay. Practice climbing the 45-foot tower with a number of climbing routes.

The Wasatch Front Rock Gym

427 West 9160 South
Sandy
801-565-3657

Teaching basic climbing skills. Kids' nights on Friday, Saturday, and Sunday from 6:30 pm - 8:30 pm. For ages 6 - 12 years old. Offers a 40-wall and boulders to climb on. Climb the crack simulator.

SCENIC DRIVES

ALPINE CANYON SCENIC LOOP

The awesome 19 miles up Alpine Canyon with numerous overlooks, grand views of waterfalls, lakes, and jagged snow-covered peaks. I-15, exit #287, east on State Hwy. 92. Fee, $3.

BIG AND LITTLE COTTONWOOD CANYONS

Big Cottonwood Canyon—stunning mountain canyon with a steep 30-mile windy climb. Offers Solitude and Brighton Ski Resorts. Little Cottonwood is just as spectacular. Snowbird and Alta Ski Resorts open year-round with dining and shopping.

CASCADE SPRING SCENIC HIGHWAY

A side road off the Alpine Canyon Scenic Loop. Seven miles long, taking you past a spring that flows down a series of limestone ledges into a pool.

NEBO SCENIC LOOP HIGHWAY

Thirty-two mile byway begins at Payson, south of Provo, down to Nephi. This is scenic high country, through Utah's mountainous terrain and is only open in the winter. At 11,877 feet, see Mt. Nebo, Utah's highest peak.

SKYLINE DRIVE

Only passable during summer months, considered the "highway to heaven." Oh, but worth the drive along the rough, unpaved road atop the Wasatch Plateau. Fifty miles long, above 10,000 feet, the views are stunning. Alpine forest surrounded by desert land. A favorite of road riders, hikers, mountain bikers, and ATV riders. Access the trail from the following cities: Mt. Pleasant, Ephraim, Spring City, and Manti. Part of the Great Western Trail.

SLEIGH RIDES & WAGON RIDES

CARRIAGE FOR HIRE

428 West 200 North, Salt Lake City 84103
801-363-8687

Reasonably priced carriage rides around Temple Square and through Memory Grove. Have them pick you up from your restaurant for an exciting evening. Up to 6 people. Half hour, $40 & $45; 1 hour, $70.

FIELDING GARR RANCH HOUSE

R & G Horse & Wagon Company
Antelope Island State Park
801-782-4946

Voted #2, the Best of Road Award as a unique attraction, offering horse-drawn wagon rides on the Island. By reservation only. See the buffalo.

HOMESTEAD BUGGY, WAGON, & CUTTER RIDES

975 West Golf Course Drive, Midway 84049
435-654-5810 888-472-7669

Take an old-fashioned sleigh pulled by majestic draft horses through beautiful snow-covered Snake Creek Valley. Or take a private sleigh ride for 2 people. Summer, wagon and buggy rides.

Private buggy & sleigh rides $22/person
Sleigh & wagon rides (up to 18 people) . $150

THIS IS THE PLACE HERITAGE PARK

2601 E. Sunnyside Avenue (800 South)
801-582-1847 www.thisistheplace.org

Step back in time at Old Deseret Village. Take a horse-drawn wagon ride through a re-created Utah pioneer village. Free with admission. Open Memorial Day - Labor Day.

SNOWBIRD SKI & SUMMER RESORT

Little Cottonwood Canyon
Snowbird 84012 801-742-2222
800-453-3000 Lodging reservations
www.snowbird.com

Ski this world-class resort.

Only 35 minutes from downtown in the scenic Little Cottonwood Canyon. Famous for its powder snow (an average 500 inches annually) and long, vertical runs. Scenic.

Children (age 12 and under) ski free if accompanied by parent. Snowboarding allowed. Four lodges, including the Cliff Lodge with spa, 13 restaurants and eateries.

Summer activities include mountain biking and hiking. With your bike, ride the tram up for a 11,000 foot descent. Concerts and festivals.

Lift & Tram Hours

Daily, weather permitting

Tram	9 am - 3:45 pm
Chairs	9 am - 4 pm
Half Days	9 am - 1 pm, 12:30 pm - 4:30 pm

Cost

All-Day, tram & chairs	$56
Chairs only	$47
Half Day, tram & chairs	$48
Half Day, chairs only	$47
Children 12 and under (with parents)	Free
Alta/Snowbird combination	$68

Directions

Take I-15 S. to I-215 E. Exit #6, 6200 S. and go right on Wasatch Blvd. Follow the signs to Little Cottonwood Canyon.

SNOWMOBILING

HIGH COUNTRY SNOWMOBILE TOURS

P.O. Box 2602
Park City 84060
435-645-7533   888-404-7669
www.highcountrysnow.com

Climb 10,000 feet on a snowmobile for a breathtaking view. Snowmobiles with handwarmers. Beginners welcome; drivers must be 16 years.

One-hour trip	$55
Three-hour lunch trip	$108
Dinner trips	$115
Half-day trip with lunch	$138
Full-day trip with lunch	$180

HOMESTEAD SNOWMOBILING

975 West Golf Course Drive
Midway 84049
435-654-5810   888-472-7669

Ride through the scenic Wasatch Mountain State Park–Snake Creek Canyon to Cascade Springs.

One Hour Ride	$50
Half-day ride with lunch	$120
Full-day ride with lunch	$155

SNOWEST SNOWMOBILES TOURS

P.O. Box 682055
Park City 84068
435-645-7669   888-499-7660
www.utahsnowmobiling.com

Snowmobile with an experience guide–beginners welcome–on a 7000-acre private ranch. Follow trails, climb hills, ride through deep powder. Children under 12 riding with their parents, free.

1 Hour (field ride only)	$48
1 Hour (mountain tour)	$78
3 Hour (mountain tour)	$98

TIMPANOGOS CAVE NATION MONUMENT

American Fork Canyon
Rural Route #3 Box 200, American Fork 84003
801-756-5238 www.nps.gov/tica

Utah's incredible caves

Plan to spend the day seeing these extraordinary caves—the Hansen, the Middle, and the Timpanogos caves. Joined by man-made tunnels.

Hike 1 1/2 hours to the caves's entrance. Wear comfortable shoes; bring food, water, and a jacket. Inside the cave, it's only 45 degrees.

Have a wonderful view of the canyons as you climb. Cavern highlights include incredible helictite formations.

Caves are open mid-May through October or when snow makes hiking difficult. In the summer, call ahead up to 30 days for a reservation. A popular activity, weekend, and holidays are especially busy.

Snack bar and picnicking facilities available.

Hours
Visitor Center

Daily (Summer)	7 am - 5:30 pm
Daily (Winter)	8:30 am - 5:00 pm

Tickets for cave tour

Daily	7 am - 4 pm

Cost

Entrance Fee per car	$3

Cave tickets

Adults	$6
Children 6 -15	$5
Children 3 - 5	$3

Directions

Located 30 minutes from Salt Lake City. Take I-15 West; exit #287 (Alpine/Highland). Go east on Hwy. 92 for 10 miles.

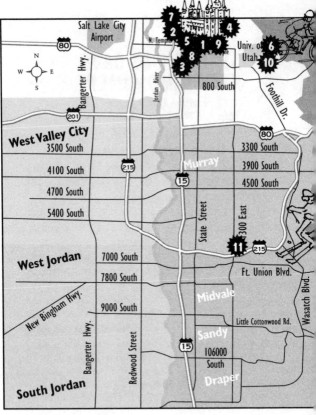

1. Brigham Young Monument
2. Children's Museum of Utah
3. Classic Cars Int'l
4. Daughters of the Utah Pioneer Museum
5. Deuel Log House
6. Fort Douglas Military Museum
7. Hill Aerospace Museum
8. Salt Lake City Art Center
9. Social Hall Heritage Museum
10. Utah Museum of Natural History
11. Wheeler Historic Farm

Salt Lake City Area

Chapter 3
HISTORIC SITES AND MUSEUMS

BRIGHAM YOUNG MONUMENT
Main and South Temple Streets

A tribute to the great Utah colonizer

Just north of Main and South Temple Streets, you find a large statue honoring the LDS Church leader, Brigham Young.

A pioneer and colonizer, Young established Salt Lake City in the mid-1800s.

The monument also pays tribute to others who helped explore and settle this valley: the fur trappers, the Indians, and those who preceded the Mormon pioneers.

Hours
24 Hours

Cost
Free

Directions
North of Main St. at South Temple St.

CHILDREN'S MUSEUM OF UTAH

840 South 300 West
Salt Lake City 84101
801-328-3383
www.childmuseum.org

Even kids can fly jumbo jets

Oh, to be a kid again. Everything's hands-on for the child in all of us. Kids pretend to operate a grocery store with shopping carts, cash registers, and more.

Fly a jetliner (a Boeing MD-11 jumbo jet). Explore a mock-up of Nine Mile Canyon. Drive a Mack truck. Plenty of activities will entertain your kids and you. See a model train display built by the Golden Spike Model Railroad Club and an elaborately decorated doll house.

Plan to take your time. Ask about their special programs, classes, and membership program. Their membership plan makes going often economical.

Hours

Mon. - Thurs.	10 am - 6 pm
Friday	10 am - 8 pm
Saturday	10 am - 6 pm

Cost

Adults & Children	$3.75
Children under 1	Free
Fridays 5 pm - 8 pm	Free

Directions

From I-15 N., exit 600 N. Go east to 300 W. Turn left on 3rd West. The museum is on the right.

CLASSIC CARS INT'L

355 West 700 South
Salt Lake City 84101
801-322-5509, 801-582-6883
www.classiccarmuseumsales.com

If you love old, classic cars—

Over 200 classic cars on display in a museum that sits on both sides of the street. The collection includes cars from 1903 to the present day, with Cadillacs, Chevys, Chryslers, and a lot more. Many rare.

Tour on your own at your pace. Photographing allowed. Plan to take your time.

Please let the museum know if you're coming after 3 pm.

Hours

Mon. - Fri . . . . 9 am - 4 pm
Saturday . . . . 9 am - 1 pm

Cost

Adults $6
Children 3 - 12 . . . . $4
Seniors $4

Directions

From I-15, exit 600 South. At the 2nd light, turn left. Go 2 blocks.

DAUGHTERS OF THE UTAH PIONEERS PIONEER MEMORIAL MUSEUM

140 East First Avenue
Salt Lake City 84103
801-538-1050

Big on pioneer artifacts

If you're particularly interested in antique dolls or Utah's history, this is an important stop.

A wonderful museum stuffed with all kinds of pioneer artifacts from 1847-1869. See the wagon that carried Brigham Young into the valley.

Guided tours available, if enough volunteer docents are on hand. Otherwise, tour on your own. Plan to take your time: four floors of paintings, china, period furniture, clothing, photographs, maps, and so much more. See old quilts, an extensive clock collection, and even an old fire engine.

Hours

Mon. - Sat. . . . . 9 am - 5 pm
Sunday (Summer only) . . . . 9 am - 1 pm

Cost

Free

Directions

On Main Street, 3 blocks north of Temple Square.

DEUEL LOG HOME

West Temple Street
Salt Lake City 84150

Picture life in pioneer days

Peek inside this old log home—it's typical of its day. Homes like these were built during the 1840s and 50s, but this particular one now serves as a reminder of this city's humble beginnings.

You'll find this old log home across from Temple Square, between the Museum of Church History and Art and the Family History Library.

Hours

Open 24 hours

Cost

Free

Directions

On West Temple St., between 35 N. and 45 N.

FORT DOUGLAS MILITARY MUSEUM

32 Potter Street
Salt Lake City
801-581-1710

Exhibits on the fort's role in Utah history

Learn how the U.S. Government built this fort in 1862 to protect the safety of the stagecoaches and the mail, but also said to be used to spy upon the Mormons.

The fort was also headquarters of the Ninth Army Command during the World War II. Now deactivated, the fort is part of the University of Utah.

Hours

Tues. - Sat. .... Noon - 4 pm

Cost

Free

Directions

Located on the east side of the University's campus, on the south side of the fort's parade grounds.

HILL AEROSPACE MUSEUM

7961 Wardleigh Road
Hill Air Force Base 84056
801-777-6818 or 801 777-7153

One of the finest collections of military aircraft

Focusing on our aerospace history–visit one of the largest museums of its kind. The collection begins with a replica the Wright brother's biplane, continuing through our present day. Sixty-four planes in all.

See missiles and ammunitions, war posters, and other interesting artifacts. Uniform room. Gift shop.

Hours

(Closed Thanksgiving, Christmas & New Year's Day)
Daily .... 9 am - 4:30 pm

Cost

Free

Directions

From I-15 N., exit #341 (Roy exit).

SALT LAKE CITY ART CENTER

20 South West Temple
Salt Lake City 84101
801-328-4201

Contemporary art museum

Salt Lake City's community art center hosts some of the finest national touring contemporary art exhibits in its lower gallery.

See exhibits of local artists with new exhibits every 6 weeks. The center offers educational classes on photography, filmmaking, and pottery in their studios. Browse through their gift shop; most items are made by local artists.

Offers Kidspace, for children ages 10 and under, where art is taught through creative projects.

Hours

Tues. - Thurs.	10 am - 5 pm
Friday	10 am - 9 pm
Saturday	1 pm - 5 pm

Cost

Free

Directions

Between the Salt Palace and Abravanel Hall.

SOCIAL HALL HERITAGE MUSEUM

51 South State Street
Salt Lake City 84111
801-321-8745

Where the pioneers went to have fun

In 1991, the whereabouts of the old Social Hall was uncovered. You find this archeological dig east of ZCMI Center Mall at the east escalators. But what are archeologists looking for? They want to find out what the early settlers of Salt Lake did for a good time. The archeological dig is at the site of the city's Social Hall, a building used for social gatherings.

The settlers forgot their hardships; they enjoyed music, dances, good food, and other fun stuff.

Guided tours available for groups.

Hours

Mon. - Fri. . . . . 10 am - 9 pm
Saturday . . . . 10 am - 7 pm

Cost

Free

Directions

Enter the museum through the walkway just east of the ZCMI Center Mall or inside the ZCMI Center Mall at the east escalators.

UTAH MUSEUM OF NATURAL HISTORY

University of Utah
1390 E. Presidents Circle (220 South)
Salt Lake City 84112
801-581-4303 801-581-6928

This museum rocks

See one of the most impressive collections of dinosaur fossils. These fossils were found regionally over the past 100 years. Also on display, see the world's largest collection of tropical turtles.

The museum is big on minerals and Utah's varied mining operations. See hundreds of rocks, a Geiger counter, and maps. On the lower level, you'll find a gift shop and a dinosaur dig for kids.

The museum is free the 1st Monday of the month. Free parking on weekends.

Once a year, attend the "What's in the Basement"? event with a curator. Learn about the museums extensive collection that's not all on display. Fun.

Hours

1st Monday of each month	Free
Mon. - Sat.	9:30 am - 5:30 pm
Sunday	Noon - 5 pm

Cost

Adults	$4
Students with ID	Free
Children 3 - 12	$2.50
Seniors	$2.50

Directions

On 220 South and University Ave.

WHEELER HISTORIC FARM

6351 South 900 East
Salt Lake City
801-264-2241
www.wheelerfarm.com

A living museum on Utah farm life

Visit this historic farm. Tour the 100-year-old historic farmhouse. Ride in the tractor-drawn wagon and milk the cow. Milk the cow every day at 5 pm except on Sunday. Plenty of farm animals.

Bring your bike and ride the farm's bike paths. Have a picnic lunch. Great place for a birthday party.

Hours

Mon. - Sat. . . . . 9 am - 5:30 pm

Cost

Farm
Free
Wagon ride
Adults/Children 3 & older $1.50
Museum House
Adults/Children 3 & older $1.50

Directions

From I-15 S., take 215 E. and exit #9. Turn left (north) on Union Park Ave. Turn left (west) 6600 S. Turn right (north) at the sign.

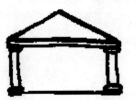

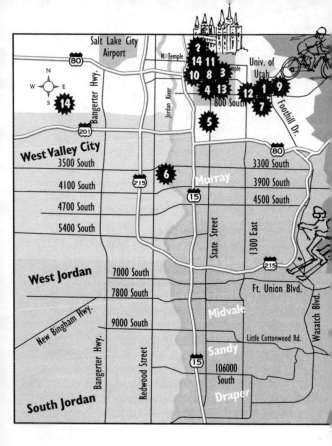

1. Babcock Theatre
2. Abravanel Hall
3. Ballet West
4. Capitol Theatre
5. Grand Theatre
6. Hale Centre Theatre
7. Kingsbury Hall

8. Off-Broadway Theatre
9. Pioneer Theatre Company
10. Repertory Dance Theatre
11. Ririe-Woodbury Dance Company
12. Salt Lake Children's Choir
13. Utah Opera
14. Utah Symphony

Salt Lake City Area

Chapter 4
SALT LAKE CITY HAS TALENT

ABRAVANEL HALL

123 West South Temple
Salt Lake City 84101
801-533-5628

Salt Lake City's Kennedy Center

Abravanel Hall's acoustic are worthy of the Metropolitan Opera House and the Kennedy Center. Rightly enough, they were designed by the same acoustic designer.

Built in the mid-70s, the hall bears the name of the symphony's former maestro Maurice Abravanel. Well-beloved, his portrait hangs in the main lobby.

Well endowed, the hall glows with its gold-leaf interior and crystal chandeliers. As you approach the hall, the mountains' reflexion appears in the huge tinted windows. Or view them as you walk down the main stairway inside.

Purchase individual tickets at the box office. Season subscribers have a special line, 801-533-6683.

Directions

Located only a few blocks from Temple Square and the Delta Center, next door
to the Salt Palace.

BABCOCK THEATRE

300 South 1340 East Street
Salt Lake City
801-581-6961

Great live theater with paying the bucks

Babcock Theatre, on the University of Utah's campus, offers student productions of a professional caliber. Their season follows the school year—from September through June. Offers 5 plays a season. See Shakespeare, as well as musicals, and other great works performed. Season tickets, $35.

Hours

Call for their performing schedule.

Cost

Individual tickets
$8 - $9

Directions

On the University of Utah's campus.

BALLET WEST

50 West 200 South
Salt Lake City 84101
801-323-6901
888-451-2787 Box Office
www.balletwest.org

This ballet's on its toes

If you thought you didn't like ballet, this exceptional ballet company may change your mind. Well-respected for their performances of classical and modern ballet.

Watch them as they perform in the classy historic Capitol Theatre. Their season runs from August through June.

Every year, they delight audiences with their holiday performances of The Nutcracker. Tickets go on sale in November.

Purchase season or individual tickets at the box office or call ArtTix, 801-355-ARTS.

Cost

Individual tickets
$10 - $45

Directions

Performances are downtown at the
Capitol Theater.

CAPITOL THEATRE

50 West 200 South
Salt Lake City 84101
801-355-2787

Gaudy is beautiful

The Capitol Theatre—originally built in 1913 for traveling vaudeville shows. Then it became the city's fanciest movie theater. But in the 1970s, the theater was restored to its orginal look. Now it is listed on the National Register of Historic Places.

Home to the Utah Opera Company and Ballet West. It hosts touring Broadway plays too.

Purchase tickets for performances at the theater's box office or by calling ArtTix, 801-355-ARTS.

Hours

Box Office

Mon. - Fri. .... 10 am - 6 pm
Saturday .... 10 am - 2 pm

Directions

Go west 1/2 block from 200 S.

GRAND THEATRE

1575 South State Street
Salt Lake City
801-957-3322

What's playing at the Grand?

Who says a students at a community college can't put on fine productions? Salt Lake City Community College has a fine reputation for sold-out preformances. Producing 6 plays a year, they present quality dramas, musicals, and comedies worthy of theater-loving families.

Students make up most of the cast, but local talent and community members love to perform here too.

Their season runs during the school year. Season tickets available. Saturday matinees. Call for their performance schedule.

Hour

Box Office

Mon. - Fri. . . . . 10 am - 6:30 pm

Cost

Individual tickets
$8.50 - $18

Directions

From downtown, travel south of State Street.

HALE CENTRE THEATRE

3333 S. Decker Lake Drive (2200 West)
West Valley City 84119
801-984-9000 Tickets
www. halecentretheatre.com

Hail to the Hale Family

For years this family-owned theater has pleased audiences with wholesome live plays, comedies, and musicals. A place to bring family members as young as 5 years of age, where they can begin to appreciate theater. Some plays return time and again as audience favorites. Once a year, the theater's founder Ruth Hale produces one of her written plays. Occasionally her family members act in plays.

Nightly shows, except on Sundays. Most Monday nights are discounted. Purchase tickets at the box office or by phone. A $2 processing fee is added to the ticket price.

Hours

Box Office

Mon. - Sat. . . . . 10 am - 7 pm
Saturday matinees . . . . Noon & 3:30 pm

Cost

Comedies

Adults . . . . $12.50 - $15.50
Children 5 - 11 . . . . $9 - $11

Musicals

Adults . . . . $14.50 - $17.50
Children 5 - 11 . . . . $11 - $13

Directions

Only 15 minutes from downtown,
East of the E Center.

77

Salt Lake City 𝒮 *Has Talent*

KINGBURY HALL

University of Utah
1350 East Presidents Circle
Salt Lake City
801-581-7100

It's all happening at Kingsbury Hall

Kingbury Hall—University of Utah's venue for student productions, national touring shows, musicals, and all kinds of entertainment. Keep up with their performing schedule. You won't want to miss out on what this theater has to offer.

Although Kingbury Hall is one of the oldest buildings on campus, it offers state-of-the-art everything. Their box office is also an ArtTix outlet, 801-355-2728.

Hour
Box Office
Mon. - Sat. . . . . 10 am - 6 pm

Cost
Varies with the show

Directions
Located on the University of Utah's campus, on the north side of Presidents Circle. From I-15, exit 600 South going east. Take 700 East going north. Then go east on 200 South.

OFF BROADWAY THEATRE

272 S. Main Street
Salt Lake City 84101
801-355-4628

Live comedy in good taste

No rehearsals, no scripts, but lots of laughs as audiences participate. Six people make up the comedy troupe "Laughing Stock." Shows open to all ages.

Also offers light-hearted, family-oriented plays, 5 to 6 a year, mostly around the holidays.

Call for schedule. Reservations accepted. Order tickets by phone through their box office.

Hours

Comedies

Friday . . . . 7:30 pm & 10 pm
Saturday . . . . 7 pm, 9 pm & 11 pm

Plays

Monday nights . . . . 7:30 pm
Thursday nights . . . . 7:30 pm
Friday nights . . . . 7:30 pm

Cost

Comedies

Adults $10
Students $8
Children under 6 . . . . $6

Plays

Monday (Family night; up to 10 people) . . $20
Thursday (any seat) $5
Friday (Ladies' night) . . . $10 (1st); Free (2nd)
Saturday . . . . Regular prices

Directions

Downtown, 2 blocks from Temple Square.

PIONEER THEATRE COMPANY

300 South 1400 East Room 205
Salt Lake City 841112
801-581-6961
www.ptc.utah.edu

Make this theater your night out on the town

Over 100,000 people attend their performances every year. Known for having quality productions. Audiences generally buy tickets well in advance. Often performances are sold out.

Producing 7 plays a year, including the classics, large-scale musicals, contemporary dramas, and comedies. Their season runs from September through June.

This fully professional theater company resides at the University of Utah and performs at the Pioneer Theatre. Tickets available at their box office. You'll find their performance schedule online.

Hours

Box Office
(Open until 8:30 pm the week before a show)
Mon. - Sat. . . . . 10 am - 6 pm

Cost

$19-$44

Directions

On campus, across from the Rice Eccles Stadium.

REPERTORY DANCE THEATRE

Rose Wagner Performing Arts Center
138 West Broadway
Salt Lake City 84101
801-534-1000
www.rdtutah.org

Extraordinary is the word

This is the 1st professional modern dance company outside New York City. Now preforming at the new Rose Wagner Performing Arts Center.

Established in 1966, the company has toured the United States and Europe extensively. Here in Utah, it offers an excellent educational program for school children.

Season and individual tickets can be purchased from ArtTix 801-355-2787. Discounts available for students and seniors.

Hours

Performance schedule online

Cost

$18

Directions

Downtown, at the Rose Wagner Performing Arts Center, next to the Historic Peery Hotel.

RIRIE-WOODBURY DANCE COMPANY

Rose Wagner Performing Arts Center
138 West Broadway
Salt Lake City 84101
801-297-4241
www.ririewoodbury.com

Salt Lake City's highly regarded dance company

Audiences the world over love this dance company's innovative approach to modern dance. Although the company has performed for over 35 years at the Capitol Theatre, they're now at the new Rose Wagner Performing Arts Center. Their season runs from September through April, offering shows for adults and children.

Every year in August, the company holds fabulous workshops for professionals, teachers, preprofessionals and teens–don't miss out.

Purchase season and individual tickets from ArtTix, 801-355-2787. Discounts available for students and seniors.

Hours
Performance schedule online

Cost
$20

Directions
Downtown, at the Rose Wagner Performing Arts Center, next to the Historic Peery Hotel.

SALT LAKE CHILDREN'S CHOIR

1033 East 300 South
Salt Lake City
801-537-1412
www.childrensing.com

Professional children's choir

Established in 1979, this childrens choir continues to gain recognition for outstanding performances, under the direction of conductor Ralph Woodward. Recently, the choir won 2nd place honors at the Golden Gate International Children's Choral Festival and Competition. Now their traveling performances are more in demand.

Occasionally, the choir performs with the Mormon Tabernacle Choir and the Utah Symphony. It has also been on PBS radio and national television.

Composing of 110 children ages 8 to 15 years, the choir rehearses weekly. Each year, among other things, they perform a free Christmas concert at the Cathedral of the Madeleine.

Although this is a children's choir, their performances are open only to those age 6 or older. Call for their performing schedule.

Hours

Performance schedules online

Cost

Free & ticketed performances

UTAH OPERA

50 West 200 South
Salt Lake City 84101
801-736-6868
www.utahopera.org

Salt Lake City has great opera

Salt Lake City's opera company produces 4 professionally staged productions a year. See them at the historic Capitol Theatre.

The company performs classical, modern, and even contemporary works. Some are locally written.

The season runs from October through May. Purchase season or individual tickets at the Capitol Theatre box office or from ArtTix, 801-355-2787. You can also buy season tickets through the mail and online.

Hours

Capitol Theatre's box office

Mon. - Fri. . . . . 10 am - 6 pm
Saturday . . . . 10 am - 2 pm

Cost

Individual tickets
$12-$57

Directions

Performances held at the Capitol Theatre,
50 W. 200 South St.

UTAH SYMPHONY

Abravanel Hall
123 W. South Temple
Salt Lake 84101
801-533-5626
www.utahsymphony.org

An Emmy Award-winning Orchestra

When this famous orchestra isn't performing at the Abravanel Concert Hall, likely it's performing somewhere in the intermountain regency. Often, the orchestra plays for schools throughout the state. It also accompanies the Utah Opera at the Capitol Theatre.

Purchase season tickets at the Abravanel Hall box office or individual tickets from ArtTix, 801-355-2787. Season subscribers call a special line, 801-533-6683.

Park at either the Crossroads Parking Garage across the street or the Delta Center Parking Garage 1/2 block away. (No validated tickets.)

Hours
Ticket Office
Mon. - Fri. .... 10 am - 6 pm
(Open until evening on concert days)
Saturday .... 10 am - 2 pm

Cost
$15-$35

Directions
Downtown. Abravanel Hall is located next to the Salt Palace and the Delta Center.

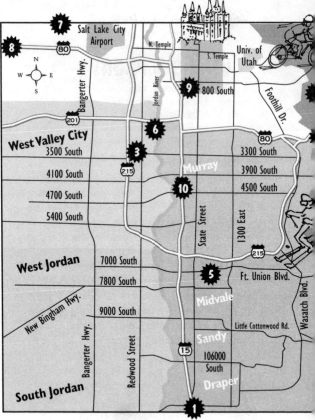

1. Glider Rides
2. Heber Valley Railroad
3. Hollywood Connections
4. Hot Air Ballooning
5. Laser Quest Salt Lake City
6. Raging Rivers
7. Salt Island Adventures
8. Skydive Salt Lake
9. Tracy Aviary
10. Utah Fun Dome

Salt Lake City Area

Chapter 5
AMUSEMENT PARKS
& ATTRACTIONS

GLIDER RIDES
Soaring Unlimited
Cedar Valley Airport

Cedar Valley
801-856-1105
www.soaringunlimited.com

A one-of-a-kind adventure with options

Soar over some of the most scenic country imaginable. You sit in the front seat with unlimited viewing, while your certified pilot sits behind you.

Offers different rides; you choose. Rides last from 20 minutes to an hour. You'll climb to 2000 feet above the valley floor to over 13,000 feet above sea level, depending on the ride.

Hours
Call for an appointment

Cost

Introductory Ride $49
Basic Sky Thrill Ride $59
The Scenic Wonder Ride $69
The Mt. Timpanogos Spectacular Ride . . $179

Directions

From downtown Salt Lake City, take I-15 South and exit #282 (Lehi). Go west to the Cedar Valley Airport Rd. about 14 miles. Turn left. Go .8 miles.

HEBER VALLEY RAILROAD

450 South 600 West
Heber City 84032
435-654-5601 or 801-581-9980
www.hebervalleyrr.org

Utah's oldest steam railroad,
the "Heber Creeper"

Step out of the comfort of your air-conditioned, smooth-riding car to another era of transportation. One of soot, cinders, and smoke, as you slowly cross scenic countryside. Dress accordingly.

Here's a living museum of railroad's golden age. Genuine steam locomotives and authentic restored coaches. These rails were constructed over 100 years ago. Trains carried goods through the valley until trucks took over in the late 1960s.

The train departs year round from Heber City and travels to Provo Canyon, for a 3- hour trip. Shorter trips are available too. Food and drinks are available on board. Coaches are heated, not air-conditioned; dress for the weather. Reservations are necessary.

Hours

Call for schedule

Cost

(Round trip)

Adults $21
Children $12
Seniors $18

Directions

Located 1 hour from Salt Lake City. Heber City is on U.S. Hwy 40 and Hwy. 189. Take I-80 east to U.S. Hwy. 40. Go south to Heber City.

HOLLYWOOD CONNECTION

3217 South Decker Lake Drive
West Valley City 84119
801-973-4FUN
www.carmike.com

New entertainment complex loaded with fun

You find all kinds of fun things to do. It's all indoors and family oriented.

Tuesdays, skate under the huge disco light to your favorite rock tunes for only $2. Thursdays, play miniature golf for just $2. Features laser tag, arcade games, and amusement rides.

Oh, and there's a 15-screen movie theater, featuring the latest first-rate movies in surround sound.

Eat at the 1950s diner that serves tasty hamburgers, fries, and extra thick milk shakes.

A popular place for birthday parties and other gatherings.

Hours

Mon. - Thurs.	3:30 pm - 10 pm
Friday	3:30 pm - Midnight
Saturday	1 pm - Midnight
Sunday	11 am - 10 pm

Cost

Individual prices for each attraction

Directions

Across from the E Center. From I-15 S. exit 3200 S. Go west. Turn right on Decker Lake Dr.

HOT AIR BALLOONING

High Adventures
5300 South 625 West Suite A-133
Park City 84123
801-301-0907 435-645-9400
www.high-adventures.com

See the countryside a whole new way. Offers half-hour ($75) and hour rides ($125). A van picks up and returns passengers to the Yarrow Hotel in Park City. Rides conclude with a traditional champagne toast, alcoholic or nonalcoholic. Reservations are a must. Early morning launches only.

Morningstar Balloons
P.O.. Box 680586
Park City 84068
435-649-9898

Offers rides year-round, weather permitting, by reservation only. Early morning flights, up to 8 people, 1/2-hour ($75) and 1-hour ($140) flights. Meet at Dan's Grocery (on Kearns Blvd.). Breakfast: orange juice and donuts. Flight ends with champagne or sparkling cider celebration.

Park City Balloon Adventures
P.O. Box 1344
Park City 84060
435-645-UPUP 800-396-8787
www.pcballoonadventures.com

Balloon rides come with a Continental breakfast—orange juice and muffins. Half-hour rides for $75 and 1-hour rides for $140. Reservations are a must; meet at the Radisson Hotel in Park City. Rides conclude with a champagne toast, alcoholic or nonalcoholic. Operates 7 days a week, early flights only.

LASER QUEST SALT LAKE CITY

7202 South 900 East
Midvale 84047
801-567-1540

See what computers do to a simple game of tag

Wander through this awesome maze, your heart pounding as you seek out your opponent in an incredible hi-tech game of tag. You're surrounded by action as the fun intensifies. You aim, you fire, you're fired upon.

Anyone big enough to wear the laser pack (children ages 6 or older) can play. Games last approximately 20 minutes.

Laser Quest is a popular activity for birthday parties, corporate groups, clubs, churches, and scout troops. Offers team building and customized games. Group discounts available.

Hours

Mon. - Thurs.	6 pm - 10 pm
Fri.	4 pm - Midnight
Sat.	Noon - Midnight
Sun.	By appointment only

Cost

Nonmember	$6.50
Members (Memberships $20)	$5
Birthday Parties per person	$10

Directions

From I-15, exit 7200 S. Go to 900 E. and go south again for 1/2 block.

RAGING WATERS

1200 West 1700 South
Salt Lake City 84104
801-972-3300

Summertime fun for families with younger kids

Definitely a great family outing if it's summer and you're a kid. Great family outing.

A small water park mostly comprises of water slides, though there is a wave pool and a large kiddie pool. And of course. It wouldn't be a water park without a lazy river for floating.

Slide, float, sunbathe, and eat; the park offers plenty of concessions: pizza, hot dogs, icy drinks, and more.

Remember that even in mid-summer, the water will be on the cool side.

Hours

Summer

Mon. - Sat. . . . . 10:30 am - 7:30 pm
Sunday . . . . Noon - 2:30 pm

Cost

Adults $16.45
Children 3 - 11 . . . . $12.95
Seniors $5.95

Directions

From I-15, exit 1700 South and go west.

SALT ISLAND ADVENTURES

Great Salt Lake South Shore
801-252-9336
www.gslcruises.com

Cruise the Great Salt Lake

Cruise the world's largest salt lake aboard the "Island Serenade." The scenic trip comes narrated with interesting tidbits about the lake's history and geology. Plenty of wildlife—bring your camera and binoculars.

Offers different types of cruises including meals. Be sure to arrive at least 15 minutes before departing.

Hours

One-Hour Scenic Cruise

Daily . . . . Noon & 1:30 pm

Six-Hour Grand Cruise (April - October)

Monthly on Saturdays . . . . 10 am - 4 pm

Cost
(Closed January & February)
One-Hour Scenic Cruise

Adults $12
Children under 12 . . . . $10
Seniors $10
Family (2 adults, 2 children) $39

Six-Hour Grand Cruise

Adults $70
Children under 12 . . . . $30
Seniors $67
Family (2 adults, 2 children) $190

Directions

Only 10 minutes from downtown. Take I-80 W. to exit #104. Follow to the Great Salt Lake State Marina. At the marina, go to the north end of the parking lot. Office in marina store.

SKYDIVE SALT LAKE

4500 North Airport Road
Erda 84074
801-255-5867 800-447-5867
www.skydivesaltlake.com

Here's a fun way to skydive

Jump with your instructor attached to you. Experience the exhilaration of free-falls. Without having to learn all the details about parachuting, take only the basic course before jumping from an airplane. A good introductory course.

Hours

Call for an appointment

Cost

Introductory Tandem Jump $155

Directions

Located 20 minutes from the Salt Lake International Airport. Take I-80 west toward Wendover. Exit #99 (Tooele), Hwy. 36. Go south to Erda Way. Go right to the airport.

TRACY AVIARY

589 East 1300 South
Salt Lake City 84105
801-596-8500
801-322-BIRD Information
www.tracyaviary.org

Birds, birds, and bird shows

In the heart of Salt Lake City. A haven for birds and bird-lovers. See over 135 different species of birds, many rare and endangered.

The aviary began in 1938, from a rich banker's private collection of birds. Today, it's one of the finest bird collections in our country. One of Salt Lake City's popular attractions.

Watch fascinating bird shows and feed the parrots during the summer. Most of the show birds were once injured or sick, but have been rehabilitated.

Hours

April - October

Daily . . . . 9 am - 6 pm

November - April

Daily . . . . 9 am - 4:30 pm

Cost

Adults $3
Children 4 - 12 & Seniors $2
Children under 5 . . . . Free
Students $2.50
Annual Gate Pass (Family) $30

Directions

Located on the south end of Liberty Park. Enter on 900 S. and 600 E. Take the one-way street past the tennis courts and swimming pool to the entrance.

UTAH FUN DOME

4998 South 360 West
Murray 84123
801-265-FUNN
www.fundome.com

One popular place for a birthday party

This huge, indoor entertainment center has what it takes to impress any kids: Magic shows, a 3-D theater, bungee jumping (8 stories high), a karaoke stage, miniature golf, arcades, go carts, bumper cars, laser tag, a double-decker carousel, and a really fun Fun House. Plus more.

Eateries offer all kinds of goodies like pizza, hot dogs, ice cream, and soft drinks. Tickets sold separately for each attraction, but purchasing a passport allows unlimited rides and other privileges.

Hours

Mon. - Thurs.	4 pm - 10 pm
Friday	4 pm - 1 am
Saturday	11 am - 1 am

Cost

Super Pass	$13.16
Extreme Super Passport	$18.81
Kids Passport	$10

Directions

In Murray, 20 minutes south of downtown. Take I-15 to the 5300 S. exit. Go west to College Dr. Go north to Murray Blvd. Turn right. Continue to Galleria Dr. Turn right and follow the signs.

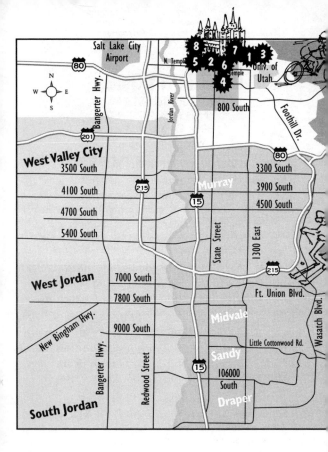

1. Cathedral of the Madeleine
2. Garden Tours
3. Governor's Mansion Tour
4. Innsbruck's City Tour
5. Latter-Day Saint Conference Center Tour
6. Latter-Day Saint Humanitarian Center Tour
7. Pioneer Trolley
8. Welfare Square

Salt Lake City Area

Chapter 6
TOURS & MORE

CATHEDRAL OF THE MADELEINE

331 East South Temple
Salt Lake City
801-328-8941

Magnificent old Romanesque cathedral with gorgeous stained-glass windows

Once you walk through the double doors, you're going to ooh and ah. This century-old, grand, elegant cathedral is well-known for its intricate stained-glass windows, made in Germany by a royal glass cutter. The cathedral is on the National Register of Historic Places.

Free tours available. The cathedral is open to the public daily, except during mass (8 am and 5:15 pm daily).

Make a self-guided tour with their $7 booklet. You can purchase it at the church office. Or simply stop in for a look.

The church has recently gone under a multimillion dollar restoration. It was built by wealthy mining families at the turn of the century, but wasn't completed until 1926.

Hours
Cathedral
Daily .... 8 am - 9 pm
Tours
Fridays .... 1 pm
Sunday .... 12:30 pm
Cost
Free
Directions
Three blocks east of Temple Square.

GARDEN TOURS

Temple Square
Salt Lake City
801-240-5916

Temple Square's awesome landscaping

Tour the lovely, ever blooming gardens surrounding the LDS Church Office Building and the Joseph Smith Memorial Building. An expert guides the tour. Learn why gardening was so important to the early pioneers.

Or tour the lush grounds of Temple Square right after the Mormon Tabernacle Choir broadcast that begins at 9:30 am on Sunday.

Learn about the history of flowers, horticulture, and how to care for your own garden.

Hours

June- September

Mon. - Sat. . . . . Noon, 2 pm, & 4 pm
Tues., Wed., & Thurs. . . . . 2 pm & 4 pm
Sunday . . . . Following the broadcast

Cost

Free

Directions

On Temple Square.

GOVERNOR'S MANSION TOUR

Kearns Mansion
603 East South Temple
Salt Lake City
801-533-0858

One magnificent old house

See one of Utah's most prestigious homes, gorgeously furnished with one of the finest collections of 18th-century period furnishings.

Tours take about 45 minutes. When you arrive, you will either join the tour in progress, or a guide will begin a new tour.

The tour takes you through the 1st floor of the mansion. See the grand hall, the formal dining room, the parlors, the butler's room and more.

The restoration of the mansion was a world-class project. It's incredible.

Hours
(July - November)

Tues. & Thurs. . . . . 2 pm - 4 pm

Cost
Free

Directions

Six blocks east of Temple Square.

INNSBRUCK'S CITY TOUR

3353 South Main Street, Suite 804
Salt Lake City
801-534-1001
www.hometown.aol.com

See it all on this tour

Tour the city's sites in the comfort of a bus with a knowledgeable guide. The tour takes you to some of the more popular attractions in and around town, including the Great Salt Lake for an extra $5.

Offers sites like Temple Square, an organ recital in the historic Tabernacle, the State Capitol building, This Is The Place Heritage Park, Olympic Village, and more.

Call ahead for a reservation and a meeting place. The bus picks up at major downtown hotels.

Hours

Daily

Departs .... 9:30 am
Returns .... 2:30 pm

Cost

$19

($5 extra for tour of the Great Salt Lake)

Directions

Call for meeting location.

LATTER-DAY-SAINT CONFERENCE CENTER TOUR

60 West North Temple
Salt Lake City
801-240-0075

Largest religious gathering center in the world

The new Latter-Day-Saint Conference Center claims state-of-the-art everything. And it seats over 21,000 people. See the original artworks of Arnold Freiberg, whose inspiring pieces were commissioned by the church.

Take the on-going, complimentary tour.

Outside, the terraced roof complex offers lush landscaping and waterfalls. There's nothing else like it. A must-see.

Hours

Daily .... 9 am - 9 pm

Cost

Free

Directions

Across from Temple Square.

LATTER-DAY SAINTS HUMANITARIAN CENTER TOUR

1665 South Bennett Road
Salt Lake City 84104
801-240-5954
801-240-6060 Reservations

See how needed supplies and food reach those in need in such a timely manner

What is the Humanitarian Center? How are they so organized? Did you know that this organization can deliver goods to needy people faster than the American Red Cross?

Take the tour. Vans leave from Temple Square on weekdays. Tours last about 2 hours.

The relief efforts of the LDS Church to victims of natural disasters and war are impressive. They clothing, food, and medical supplies to the needy throughout the world within days. Food items come from the church's Welfare Square and donations.

See workers sorting used clothing; watch the video. A must-do.

Hours
(Weather permitting)
Daily . . . . 10 am, Noon, and 2 pm
Evening tours
Tues., Wed., & Thurs. . 6:30 pm, 7 pm, 7:30 pm

Cost
Free

Directions
Meet at Temple Square's west gate.

PIONEER TROLLY

Temple Square
Salt Lake City
801-240-6279

Don't walk when you can take the trolley

Hop aboard this trolley for a 15-minute, narrated ride of some of the LDS Church sites. The different stops include the Beehive House, the Joseph Smith Memorial Building, Temple Square, the new Conference Center, the Relief Society Building, and the Church Office Building.

Each site's significance will be explained in detail.

Hours
(Summers only)
Mon. - Sat. .... 10 am - 4 pm

Cost
Free
Directions
Pick up the trolley along Temple Square.

WELFARE SQUARE

800 South 800 West
Salt Lake City
801-240-7332

One of the most interesting tours in Salt Lake City

This no-frills tour lets you peer into the heart of the Church's welfare system. Learn how this church takes care of its needy—those who are unable to provide for themselves.

This system is so unique, yet so efficient, that you'll leave feeling impressed. See the cannery, the bakery, the storehouses, and more.

Tours start at the facility's visitor center and last about 45 minutes. The last tour of the day begins at 2:30 pm.

Hours
(Tours)
Mon. - Fri. . . . . 10 am - 2:30 pm
(The facility closes at 4 pm)

Cost
Free

Directions

From Temple Square, simply go south to 800 S. and west to 800 W. The center is on the south corner.

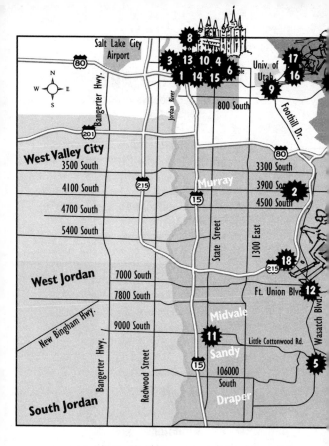

1. Big City Soup
2. Cafe Madrid
3. Diamond Lil's
4. The Garden
5. La Caille
6. Lion House Pantry
7. Log Haven
8. Mandarin Restaurant
9. Market St. Broiler

10. Market St. Grille
11. Mayan Restaurant
12. Porcupine Grille
13. Red Iguana
14. Rio Grande Cafe
15. The Roof
16. Ruth's Diner
17. Santa Fe
18. Tuscany

Salt Lake City Area

Chapter 7
EATING OUT IN SALT LAKE CITY

BIG CITY SOUP

235 South 400 West
Salt Lake City 84102
801-333-7687
www.bigcitysoup.com

Gourmet soups

Hot flavorful soups on a chilly day makes this eatery a real winner. Gourmet soups are their specialty and the Thai chicken Noodle, the Boston clam chowder, the rock crab and roma tomato, the crab and brie, and the white bean and Italian sausage soups are some favorites.

Sample the soups before you pick the one you want. Your choice of soup—about 16 soups in all comes with freshly baked Volker's bread and a hunk of cheese, making it a dandy lunch. Here's a healthy alternative to fast food.

Find their daily specials posted on the web. Serving lunch only. Excellent for take-outs; soups by the quart.

Hours

Mon. - Sat. . . . . 11 am - 3 pm

Cost

Bowl of soup . . . .$5 - $7

Directions

From I-15 S., exit 600 S. Go north on 400 W.

CAFE MADRID

2080 East 3900 South
Salt Lake City 84124
801-273-0837

Spanish

Off the beaten track in an old abandoned strip mall in Holladay, this restaurant's Spanish cuisine promises to take your taste buds on an culinary adventure without paying airfare.

Small. Completely casual. Offers a cozy, but lively atmosphere, like you'd find in Spain. Great outdoor patio dining. Exciting tapas. Excellent paella (order 24 hours in advance). Entrees include black Angus tenderloin in Roquefort sauce and lamb shank in port wine sauce (with baby carrots, onions, and mushrooms). Game in season.

Serving dinner only; call for reservations particularly on weekends.

Hours

Tues. - Sat. .... 5:30 pm - closing

Cost

$14 - $22

Directions

In Holladay. From downtown, go east on 400 S, then go south on 700 E. Turn east on 3900 S.

DIAMOND LIL'S RESTAURANT

1528 West North Temple
Salt Lake City 84116
801-533-0547

Steakhouse

A down-home eatry. Famous for their prime rib that doesn't come any more succulent. Excellent for great steaks, halibut, salmon, crab, and chicken dishes too. Serves tasty cordon bleu. But your meal isn't over until you've tried their yummy homemade pie. Little atmosphere.

Stop in for lunch or dinner; open for dinner only on Saturdays. Closed on Sundays. Come dressed as you are.

Hours
Lunch
Mon. - Fri. . . . . 11 am - 4 pm
Dinner
Mon. - Sat. . . . . 4 pm - 10 pm

Cost
Prime Rib . . . . $14.99 & up

Directions
Only 5 minutes from Temple Square
on North Temple.

THE GARDEN RESTAURANT

Joseph Smith Memorial Building
15 East South Temple, (10th Floor)
Salt Lake City 84111
801-539-1911

American

Enjoy a splendid view of the valley from the 10th floor of the Joseph Smith Memorial building. The restaurant's retractable glass roof provides open-air dining, and the garden makes it lovely any day.

The food's delicious with choices of salads, sandwiches, pasta dishes, and a few entrees, but the Oriental Chicken Pasta Salad—their signature salad—is what people crave the most. A new dessert daily.

There's no shortage of nice things to drink, although the restaurant doesn't serve coffee or alcoholic beverages.

Great for out-of-town guests and quiet conversations. Reservations accepted for groups of 8 or more.

Hours

Lunch
Mon. - Sat. . . . . 11 am - 3:30 pm

Dinner
Mon. - Sat. . . . . 5 pm - 10 pm

Cost

Lunch . . . . $8 - $16
Dinner . . . . $12 - $19

Directions

Atop the Joseph Smith Memorial Building.

LA CAILLE

9565 South Wasatch Boulevard
Sandy 84092
801-942-1751

European

Salt Lake City's finest and most romantic restaurants, located in a beautiful setting in Little Cottonwood Canyon. Eat at a French country chateau with a luxurious European menu. Dinner served nightly. Sunday brunch.

You'll find this place stunning, including the prices. But if you want impressive, here's your restaurant.

Hours

Mon. - Sat. . . . . 6 pm - 9 pm
Sunday Brunch . . . . 10 am - 1 pm
Sunday Family Style Meal . . . . 6 pm - 9 pm

Cost

$39 - $63

Directions

Take 400 South going east; it will become Foothill Blvd. Then take I-215 S. and exit #6 (6200 S.). Go east. The road becomes Wasatch Blvd. Continue 4 miles until you reach a fork in the road. Watch for the restaurant's sign directing you to go right, continuing (on Wasatch Blvd.) for about 1 mile. The restaurant is on the east side of the road. Look for the large gates and red brick lane.

LION HOUSE PANTRY RESTARUANT

63 East Temple
Salt Lake City 84105
801-363-5466 www.lion-house.com

American

A visit to Temple Square should include lunch at Brigham Young's historic mansion, the Lion House. The house's early 1900s charm makes the perfect place to serve up dishes with a local heritage. If Utah has its own cuisine, this would be it.

Although Brigham Young is no longer the host, he managed to leave some the early 20th-century comforts we all crave. Food is priced al carte. Reservations accepted.

Hours

Lunch
Mon. - Fri. . . . . 11 am - 2 pm
Dinner
Thurs. - Sat. . . . . 5 pm - 8:30 pm

Cost

Lunch . . . . $5 - $15
Dinner . . . . $7 - $18

Directions

A half-block east of Temple Square.

LOG HAVEN

3800 South Wasatch Boulevard
Salt Lake City 84109
801-272-8255

Contemporary

A truly enchanting evening awaits you at this rustic, yet elegant, restaurant in the canyon. Gaze out the large windows at scenic waterfalls and wildflowers. Surrounded with pine trees, the restaurant's only minutes from downtown. Summertime is a treat with their outdoor dining.

The menu's sophisticated and changes seasonally, so you can never go too often. Wonderful desserts too. Reservations required.

Hours

Daily .... 5 pm - about 10 pm

Cost

$17-$32

Directions

Four miles up Mill Creek Canyon, on the left.

MANDARIN RESTAURANT

348 East 900 North
Bountiful 84010
801-298-2406 www.mandarinutah.com

Chinese

Voted "Best of Utah" and one of the "Top 25 Chinese Restaurants in the U.S." their Chinese food here is that good. This restaurant's has won as impressive list of awards.

Opened in 1978, the restaurant draws people from all over the Wasatch Front. Each dish they serve receives special attention. Known for their exquisite sauces and weekly specials.

Reservations are accepted for groups of 8 people or more–Monday through Thursday only.

Hours

Mon. - Thurs. . . . . 5 pm - 9:30 pm
Fri. & Sat. . . . . 5 pm - 10:30 pm

Cost

$15-$30

Directions

From Salt Lake City, take I-15 N. to Bountiful (about 10 miles). Exit #321 on 400 N. Bountiful. Travel east to 400 E. Turn left and go north 2 blks. The restaurant is on the corner of 900 N. and 400 E.

MARKET STREET BROILER

260 South 1300 East
Salt Lake City 84102
801-583-8808 www.gastronomyinc.com

Seafood

Three in one—it's the Market Street Broiler, a fish market, and the deli, located in an old fire station. Their fish is flown in daily and the restaurant broils the fresh fish over mesquite, making it delicious. Popular for their exceptional clam chowder and hickory smoked barbecued ribs. Sandwiches and salads.

Hours

Lunch

Mon. - Sat.	11 am - 4 pm
Sunday (Summer)	11 am - 4 pm

Dinner

Mon. - Thurs.	4 pm - 10 pm
Fri. - Sat.	4 pm - 10:30 pm
Sunday	4 pm - 9 pm

Cost

Lunch	$5 - $32
Dinner	$10 - $33

Directions

Only 5 minutes from downtown. Located inside the historic Fire Station #8 near the University of Utah, on Salt Lake City's east bench.

MARKET STREET GRILL

48 W. Market Street
Salt Lake City 84101
801-322-4668 www.gastronomyinc.com

Seafood

Salt Lake City's top restaurant when it comes to seafood. Offers fresh fish flown in daily from around the world. Famous for their exceptional clam chowder and their creamy Caesar dressing. The restaurant also serves certified Angus beef and chicken.

An excellent place for breakfast, serving seafood omelettes as well as more traditional items.

Hours
Breakfast
Mon.-Fri .... 6:30 am - 11 am
Saturday .... 7 am - Noon
Lunch
Mon. - Fri. .... 11 am - 3 pm
Saturday .... Noon - 3 pm
Dinner
Mon. - Thurs. .... 3 pm - 10 pm
Fri. - Sat. .... 3 pm - 11 pm
Sunday .... 3 pm - 9:30 pm
Sunday Brunch
Sundays .... 9 am - 3 pm
Cost
Breakfast $5 - $10; Lunch $6-$18; Dinner $14-$52
Directions
Market St. is located at 350 S.,
between Main & W. Temple Sts.

Cottonwood location:
2985 East 6580 South
Salt Lake City 84121
801-942-8860

MAYAN RESTAURANT

9400 South State Street
Salt Lake City 84070
801-304-4677   www.jordancommons.com

Mexican

Watch the amazing cliff divers dive off 30-foot waterfalls at this Disneyland-like Mexican restaurant. Divers perform every 40 minutes. This elaborate restaurant resembles an ancient Mayan ruin. The Mexican cuisine served here includes shrimp tacos, fajitas, and a tasty taco salad. More than just eating out, it's an adventure–bring the kids.

Located in the Jordon Commons complex where you'll also find a 16-screen movie theater and the 70 mm Cricket Super Screen, the largest movie screen in Utah. So enjoy plenty of entertainment.

Hours

Daily . . . . 11 am - 10 pm

Cost

$6 - $14

Directions

From I-15 S., exit 9000 South.

PORCUPINE PUB & GRILLE

3698 East Fort Union Boulevard
Salt Lake City 84121
801-942-5555

Pizza

Conveniently located near the mouth of Big Cottonwood Canyon, this popular restaurant's a hit with hungry skiers, hikers, and mountain bikers. The restaurant is ready with hefty portions of food, serving piping-hot chili, pizza, and their famous fish and chips, made from fresh halibut flown in daily, and cooked up fresh. Other yummy eats include their stacked chicken enchiladas covered with pepper mole sauce and black bean burritos.

Dinner entrees. Offers a weekend brunch both Saturday and Sunday.

Hours

Mon. - Sat. . . . . 11 am - 11 pm
Sunday . . . . 9 am - 10 pm

Cost

Fish & Chips (Lunch) $9.99
Dinner entrees . . . . $13 - $24

Directions

Located above the Lift House Ski Shop, on the southeast corner of Wasatch and Fort Union Blvds.

RED IGUANA

736 West North Temple
Salt Lake City 84116
801-322-1489

Mexican

Absolutely the best Mexican food in town at this unpretentious little diner. Only 5 minutes from Temple Square. People love their authentic Mexican dishes— many are exotic dishes from different parts of Mexico. Popular for their award-winning mole—an exotic sauce for meats that combines chilis and chocolate— they're often referred to as "Mole Kings." Enchiladas, burritos, steaks, and more. Dishes come with rice, beans, and your choice of tortillas. Family owned and operated.

Hours

Mon. - Wed.	11 am - 9 pm
Fri., & Sat.	11 am - 10 pm
Sunday	Noon - 9 pm

Cost

$5 - $20

Directions

From downtown, take N. Temple to 736 W. or take I-80 W. to the Redwood Rd. exit. Then go north to N. Temple, turn right, then go east to 736 W.

RIO GRANDE CAFE

270 South Rio Grande (455 West)
Salt Lake City 84101
801-364-3302

Mexican

Although the cafe's location is in a somewhat less desirable side of downtown, their tasty Mexican food gives good reason to go there.

The menu's simple; traditional tacos, enchiladas, burritos, and more. Excellent Mexican-style steaks too. The famous "carnitas" is served only after 5 pm. Offers the best nachos in town. Their super burritos are also popular–as weekly specials.

The cafe's a hotspot for event-goers.

Hours

Lunch

Mon. - Fri.	11 am - 2:30 pm
Saturday	11:30 am - 2:30 pm

Dinner

Mon. - Thurs.	5 pm - 9:30 pm
Fri. - Sat.	5 pm - 10:30 pm
Sunday	4 pm - 9 pm

Cost

Lunch	$5 - $15
Dinner	$7 - $18

Directions

Inside the Rio Grand train depot.

THE ROOF RESTAURANT

Joseph Smith Memorial Building
15 East South Temple (10th Floor)
Salt Lake City 84111
801-539-1911 wwwjsmb.com

American

A gourmet buffet? Yes. An elegant feast fit for a king. Eat some of the tastiest desserts in town; enjoy the view from atop the Joseph Smith Memorial Building.

Open only for dinner; closed on Sundays. Reservations are wise, especially on weekends. LDS-Church owned and operated, so no coffee, tea, or alcoholic drinks are served.

How about dinner and a show? Watch the show, *Testaments,* playing below in the Legacy Theater. Free admission. Pick up your tickets in advance.

Hours

Dinner only

Mon. - Thurs. . . . . 5 pm - 9 pm
Fri. & Sat. 5 pm - 10 pm

Cost

$26.95

Directions

On the 10th floor of the Joseph Smith Memorial Building, across from Temple Square.

RUTH'S DINER

210 Emigration Canyon Road
Salt Lake City 84108 801-582-5807

American

A diner in old trolley car is now a Salt Lake City legend. Best brunch and breakfast in town. It serves a great all-day breakfast including good-tasting huevos rancheros and Ruth's yummy biscuits and raspberry jam. Sunday brunch is always crowded.

Features the ever-popular teriyaki chicken, meatloaf, and pot roast. Burgers, fries, and salads. The house dessert—the hot fudge brownie sundae—comes smothered in Ruth's fudge sauce with real whipped cream, a cherry, and a scoop of Snelgrove's vanilla ice cream. Sinful.

Insider's tip: Eat here in the summertime, on their 3-tiered patio overlooking the creek, listen to live music played on weekends. Enjoyable.

Nearby there's the Hogle Zoo and This Is The Place Heritage Park.

Cost
Breakfast .... $4 - $6
Lunch .... $6 - $9
Dinner .... $8 - $10

Hours
(Open every day until 10 pm in the summer)
Mon. - Thurs. .... 8 am - 9 pm
Fri. & Sat. .... 8 am - 10 pm
Sunday .... 8 am - 10 pm

Directions
Take 800 S. towards the mountains. The road becomes Sunnyside Ave. Go up the canyon almost 2 miles; the restaurant is on the right.

SANTA FE RESTAURANT

2100 Emigration Canyon
Salt Lake City 84108
801-582-5888
www.cuiscenery.com

Southwestern

Another finest of Salt Lake City restaurant with a main upstairs dining room with a floor-to-ceiling stained glass wall, picturing one of Utah's red rock canyons and a patio, overlooking scenic Emigration Creek.

Signature dishes awaiting your taste buds include the double-cut grilled pork chop with an apple jack glaze and sweet potato home fries or the baby back ribs with sweet, spicy mango-chipotle barbecue sauce. The Pasilla Spiced Shrimp is always a favorite. So is the flank steak. Offering seasonal dishes.

Hours

Mon. - Sat. . . . . 5 pm - 10 pm
Sunday . . . . 4 pm - 9 pm
Sunday Brunch . . . . 10 am - 2:30 pm

Cost

Entrees . . . . $8.45 - $19.95

Directions

At the mouth of Emigration Canyon. Take 800 South going east towards the mountains. The street will become Sunnyside Avenue.

TUSCANY

2832 East 6200 South
Salt Lake City 84121
801-277-9919
www.tuscanyslc.com

Italian

A delectable Italian cuisine served in a mountain lodge at the foot of the Wasatch Mountains. Tops for scenic outdoor dining. Tops for its award-winning Sunday brunch, including power waffles (made with yogurt, whole grains, and molasses, piled with fresh fruit), custom-made omelettes, baked sugar ham, and freshly baked desserts.

House specialities: Grilled Pacific Pesto-Crusted Salmon served with toasted vegetable couscous and Hardwood Grilled Double Cut Pork Chop with scallion mashed potatoes. Delicious baked crusty Italian style peasant breads, calzoni, and pasta dishes.

Hours

Lunch
Tues. - Fri. . . . . 11:30 am - 2:30 pm
Sunday . . . . 10 am - 2 pm

Dinner
Mon. - Thurs. . . . . 5 pm - 9:45pm
Fri. & Sat. . . . . 5 pm - 10:30 pm
Sunday . . . . 5 pm - 9 pm

Cost

Lunch . . . . $8.95 - $13.95
Dinner entree . . . . $14.95 - $28.95
Sunday brunch (Adult) $17.95

Directions

From downtown, take I-15 S. to I-215 E. Exit 6200 S. Go west on 6200 S. The restaurant is 1 block down on the left.

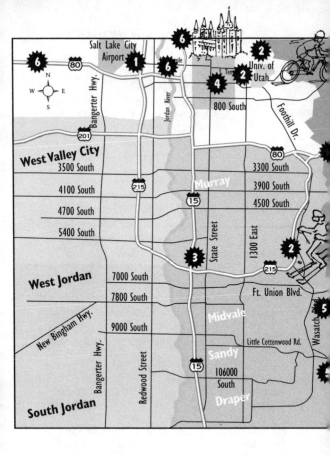

1. Salt Lake Airport Hotels
2. Salt Lake City Bed & Breakfast and Inns
3. Salt Lake City Central/Valley Inns
4. Salt Lake City Downtown Hotels
5. Resorts
6. RV Parks and Campgrounds

Salt Lake City Area

Chapter 8
WHERE TO STAY ?

Where to Stay?

SALT LAKE CITY AIRPORT

HILTON SALT LAKE CITY AIRPORT

5151 Wiley Post Way, Salt Lake City 84116
801-539-1515 800-999-3736 www.hilton.com

Recently renovated, this 287-room hotel sits waterfront in a business park. Offers a putting green and running path. Only 2 miles from the airport, free airport shuttle. Includes free parking, a swimming pool, a fitness center, a sports court, a hot tub, and a restaurant with a view. Suites for business people and suites with jetted sunken tubs. Even a Presidential suite. From the airport, take I-80 W., exit #114. At the 2nd light, turn left. Rates at $99.

HOLIDAY INN EXPRESS AIRPORT EAST

2080 West North Temple, Salt Lake City 84116
801-355-0088 800-465-4329 www.hiexpress.com

Newly renovated; reasonably priced, located between downtown and the airport. Includes free 24-hour airport shuttles, free parking, free deluxe breakfast, and free local calls. Laundry service, an indoor Jacuzzi, premium TV, ski storage, and a shuttle to downtown, for a fee. Suites with microwaves and refrigerators. Rates at $65.

RADISSON HOTEL SALT LAKE CITY AIRPORT

2177 West North Temple, Salt Lake City 84116
801-364-5800 800-333-3333 www.radisson.com

Highly rated (AAA 4-Diamond) luxury hotel. Only 3 minutes from airport. Free airport shuttle, free deluxe Continental breakfast, free local calls, and free covered parking. Oversized rooms with refrigerators. Suites with fireplaces, kitchens, balconies, and lofts. Outdoor heated pool, whirlpool spa, and fitness room. Rates at $69.

RESIDENCE INN BY MARRIOTT
SALT LAKE CITY AIRPORT

4883 West Douglas Corrigan Way
Salt Lake City 84116
801-532-4101 800-331-3131
www.residenceinn.com

New. Only a mile from the airport. Studios or suites, both with kitchens. Free breakfast buffet and free airport shuttle. Includes a fitness center, ski lockers, a whirlpool, and an indoor pool. Free parking. From I-80 W., exit #114. Rates at $79.

SKY HARBOR SUITES

1876 West North Temple, Salt Lake City 84116
801-539-8420 800-677-8483

Very nice. Homey. Highly rated hotel (AAA 3-Diamond) offering suites with full kitchens, cable TV, and free local calls. The list of amenities includes a fitness center, spas, a tennis court, a sauna, a pool, a business center, and free airport shuttles. Easy freeway access. Ideal for extended stays or short visits. Offers studios, lofts, 1 and 2 bedroom units. Call for reservations. Rates at $83.

SUPER 8 MOTEL SALT LAKE CITY AIRPORT

223 North Jimmy Doolittle Road
Salt Lake City 84116
801-533-8878 www.super8.com

Nice. An award-winning budget hotel, about 5 years old, that's ideal for families, business people, and skiers looking for a bargain stay. Offers Jacuzzi suite, free Continental breakfasts, a whirlpool, a laundry facility, and free airport shuttles. From the airport, take I-80 West, exit #114. Rates at $70.

SALT LAKE CITY
BED & BREAKFAST AND INNS

ARMSTRONG MANSION
HISTORIC BED & BREAKFAST

667 East 100 South, Salt Lake City 84102
801-531-1333 800-524-5511
www.armstrong-bb.com

Elegant, Queen Anne-style mansion with 13 suites, each with a private bath. Only 7 blocks from downtown. Also a gourmet breakfast every morning. Freshly-made cookies and cider in your room. Cable TV and complimentary movies. Free parking. Call for reservations. Rates $99-$229.

BRIGHAM STREET INN

1135 East South Temple, Salt Lake City 84102
801-364-4461 800-417-4461

A real Salt Lake treat, very upscale, Stay in a historic Victorian house listed on the National Historic Register. Offers 8 beautifully decorated rooms and 1 large suite with jetted tub. Highly rated with 4 Stars Mobil, AAA 4 Diamonds. Waffles, pastries, and fresh fruit in the morning. No smoking. Free parking. Call for reservations. Rooms at $185.

LOG CABIN ON THE HILL

2275 East 6200 South
Holladay 84121 801-272-2969

Rustic, cozy, 65-year-old log cabin. A great mountain getaway that's popular with skiers and couples, because of its proximity to local resorts and the mountains. Four comfortable rooms with antiques and fancy rugs. Homestyle breakfasts. Kids allowed. Call for reservations. Rates $95-$105.

SALT LAKE CITY CENTRAL/VALLEY

CRYSTAL INN MIDVALLEY

818 East Winchester Street, Murray 84119
801-736-2000 www.crystalinns.com

Affordable, yet nice amenities. Includes free hot buffet breakfast, free airport shuttles, a whirlpool spa, a fitness center, a heated indoor pool, and Jacuzzi suites. Rooms with two phone lines, microwaves, refrigerators, cable TV, and movie rentals. Kids stay free. Easy accessibility to Big and Little Cottonwood ski resorts. From I-215, exit #9, Union Park Avenue. Weekends $59; weekdays $89.

HOMEWOOD SUITES

844 East North Union Avenue, Midvale 84047
801-561-5999 www.hilton.com

Roomy 1 and 2 bedroom suites with fully equipped kitchens. Some suites with fireplace. Hot breakfasts. Close to restaurants and shopping. Only 30 minutes from ski resorts and 20 minutes from downtown. From downtown, take I-15 S. to I-215 E. and exit #9 (Union Park Ave.). Go south to Fort Union. Turn right; go two lights. Weekends $79; weekdays $119-$129.

QUALITY INN MIDVALE

4465 Century Drive, Salt Lake City 84124
801-268-2533 800-268-5801 w.sunbursthospitality.com

Hot tub suites. Free Continental deluxe breakfasts. Easy accessibility to ski resorts. Offers 131 rooms with HBO, an outdoor pool, and a great mountain view. AAA rating. Starting at $49.95.

RESIDENCE INN BY MARRIOTT, COTTONWOODS

6425 South 3000 East, Salt Lake City 84121
801-453-0430 800-331-3131
www.residenceinn.com

Location makes this hotel attractive to skiers. Convenient to the Cottonwood ski resorts, yet only minutes away from downtown. The hotel is also across from the Old Mill Golf Course. Offers 1 and 2 bedroom suites with kitchens and sitting areas. Guests enjoy a hearty complimentary breakfast every morning. Starting at $69.

RESTON HOTEL

5335 College Drive, Murray 84123
801-264-1054 800-231-9710
www.restonhotelslc.com

This elegant, 98-room hotel is reasonably priced and has great proximity to skiing and sightseeing. Free Continental breakfasts, free local calls, cable TV, HBO, an indoor heated pool, and a whirlpool spa. From I-15, exit #303 (5300 S.). Starting at $71.

SUGAR HOUSE VILLAGE ALL SUITE INN

1339 East 2100 South, Salt Lake City 84105
801486-9976 888-577-8483
www.sugarhousevillage.com

Affordable rate. Great for vacationing families and for extended stays. Large, roomy suites within easy access of ski resorts and downtown. Cable TV, playground, hot tub, laundry facility, and barbecue grills. Small dogs allowed. Starting at $79.

SALT LAKE CITY DOWNTOWN

CRYSTAL INN DOWNTOWN

230 West 500 South, Salt Lake City 84101
801-328-4466 www.crystalinns.com

Bargain prices, nice large rooms. Suites with microwaves, refrigerators, 2 phone lines, free local calls, fitness center, whirlpool, sauna, and indoor pool. Free hot buffet breakfasts. Kids stay free. Close to Temple Square. TRAX 2 blocks. Starting at $69-$89.

GRAND AMERICA HOTEL

555 South Main Street, Salt Lake City 84111
801-258-6000 www.grandamerica.com

Very upscale. Rooms or suites with floor-to-ceiling windows overlooking the city. The 24-story hotel offers room service, cable TV, HBO, an indoor, heated pool, a restaurant, and free parking. Kids stay free. TRAX stops in front. Weekends $65; weekdays $79.

HILTON SALT LAKE CITY CENTER

255 South West Temple, Salt Lake City 84101
801-328-2000 www.hilton.com

A 499-room hotel with nice downtown location, underground parking, an indoor pool, a fitness center, a Jacuzzi, room service, a business center, and two restaurants. Kids stay free. Small pets. TRAX 1/2 block away. Starting at $79-$89.

HISTORIC PEERY HOTEL

110 West Broadway, Salt Lake City 84101
801-521-4300 800-331-0073 ww.peeryhotel.com

Like Europe. An old historic, 73-room hotel, completely renovated. Nice rates, great amenities: valet parking, room service, a fitness center, a whirlpool, free breakfast, and free airport shuttle. Kids stay free. On the National Register. TRAX 1-1/2 blocks $102.

HOTEL MONACO

15 West 5200 South, Salt Lake City 84101
801-595-0000   877-294-9710
www.monaco-saltlakecity.com

A fun, luxury "boutique" hotel housed in old downtown bank building. Pet friendly—so bring yours. Guests can adopt one of their goldfish and have it in their rooms. Sweet on amenities: valet parking, laundry service, a fitness center, and a complimentary massage. Kids stay free. Close to Temple Square. TRAX stops in front. Rooms at $92 weekends; $129-$159 weekdays.

INN AT TEMPLE SQUARE

71 West South Temple, Salt Lake City 84101
801-531-1000   800-843-4668   www.theinn.com

Close to Temple Square and all the other downtown attractions. Offers an elegant restaurant, "Passages," valet parking, free local calls, free buffet breakfast, and a small lending library. The LDS-Church-owned hotel includes rooms with 4-post beds and refrigerators with sodas. No smoking. Kids stay free. TRAX stops in front. Complimentary valet parking. Rates at $98 weekends; $115-$130 weekdays.

LITTLE AMERICA HOTEL & TOWER

500 South Main Street, Salt Lake City 84101
801-363-6781   www.littleamerica.com

Two hotels in one offer nicely appointed rooms at bargain prices or the more pricey luxurious suites. Nice amenities. Excellent restaurant. One of the city's great places for overnight hospitality. Free parking. Kids stay free.. TRAX 1/2 block away. Rates start at Hotel, $65 - $79; Tower, $99-$170 .

SALT LAKE CITY MARRIOTT CITY CENTER
220 South State Street, Salt Lake City 84111
801-961-8700 www.saltlakecitymarriott.com
New. The Marriott's hottest hotel offers a great location for sightseeing, skiing, and business travel. Great weekend rates, and free airport shuttles. Kids stay free. Covered parking, valet parking. TRAX one block away. Rates at $79 weekends; $159 weekdays.

SHERATON CITY CENTRE HOTEL
150 West 500 South, Salt Lake City 84101
801-401-2000 www.sheraton.com
Excellent overall location to Salt Lake City's best attractions—Temple Square, ski resorts, and shopping. TRAX 1-1/2 blocks away. Kids stay free. Rates at $79 weekends, $89 weekdays.

WESTCOAST SALT LAKE HOTEL
161 West 600 South, Salt Lake City 84101
801-521-7373 800-325-4000
Near the Salt Palace, Temple Square, the Delta Center, and shopping. Low rates and nice amenities: cable TV, room service, a laundry facility, a whirlpool, a pool, a free airport shuttle, a business center, and a fitness center. Best of all, free parking. Kids stay free. TRAX 1-1/2 blocks away. Small pets allowed. Rates at $89 weekends; $139 weekdays.

WYNDHAM HOTEL
215 West South Temple, Salt Lake City 84101
801-531-7500 www.wyndham.com/saltlakecity
Only a block from Temple Square, this hotel offers quality without being pricey. An indoor heated pool, an exercise room, a whirlpool spa, and a restaurant. Free airport shuttles. Kids stay free. TRAX in front. Rates at $79 weekends; $139 weekdays.

RESORTS
ALTA LODGE
P.O. Box 8040, Alta 84092
801-742-3500 800-707-2582 Reservations
www.altalodge.com

Built in 1939, newly renovated–a skier's haven and summer retreat. Dorms, rooms, and 2-bedroom condo. Some units with fireplaces. Included in your stay: breakfast, dinner, and lift tickets. Hot pools, heated outdoor pool, sun deck. No TVs in rooms. Excellent food at Alta Lodge Dining Room (winter only), open to the public by reservation, Sunday brunch (year round). Shuttle service to Alta's base area & Snowbird Ski Resort. Hiking and mountain biking in the summer.

ALTA PERUVIAN LODGE
P.O. Box 8017, Alta 84092
801-742-3000 www.altaperuvian.com

An old world ski lodge. A stay here includes lodging, meals, and lift passes. Offers dorms, rooms, chalets, and suites. Heated outdoor pool, sauna, nightly movies, best-seller library. Ski shop with rentals. Shuttle service to Alta's base area & Snowbird Ski Resort.

ALTA RUSTLER LODGE
P.O. Box 8030, Alta 84092
801-742-2200 888-532-2582 Reservations
ww.altarustlerlodge.com

One of the nicest places to stay in the Canyon. Rooms come with cable TV, heated pool, Jacuzzi, and exercise center. Popular place for a Sunday brunch. Ski lift within walking distance.

ALTA'S SNOWPINE LODGE

Little Cottonwood Canyon
Alta 84092 801-742-2000

Family operated; open winters only. Western-looking elegant lodge with dorms, rooms, and dining hall. An overnight stay includes breakfast, dinner, and lift tickets. Excellent cuisine. Dining area open to the public by reservation only. Outdoor heated pool, Jacuzzi, sauna, and a ski lift right out the door. Free shuttle to Snowbird ski resort. Open in winter only.

BRIGHTON CHALETS

Brighton Loop Road
801-942-8824
www.brightonchalets.com

Have your own personal chalet in the beautiful mountains where you can catch the ski lift practically at your doorstep. Marvelous for summer, when fishing and hiking are the attractions. Offers kitchens, barbecues, fireplaces, whirlpool baths, and dishTV.

SNOWBIRD SKI & SUMMER RESORT, THE CLIFF LODGE

P.O. Box 929000
Snowbird 84092
801-933-2222   www.snowbird.com

Only 29 miles to the airport with 348 rooms that have cable TV. The lodge has a rooftop pool, spa, and a fitness facilities. Good restaurants.

SOLITUDE MOUNTAIN RESORT

P.O. Box 929000
Snowbird 84092 801-933-2222
www.skisolitude.com

You don't have to ski to enjoy the resort—offers an inn or 1 - 4 bedrooms condominiums. Cable TV, hot tub, pool. Located at the ski base.

RV PARKS AND CAMPGROUND

HIDDEN HAVEN CAMPGROUND

2200 Rasmussen Road
Park City 84098
435-649-8935

Only minutes from Salt Lake City. Secluded campground with grassy area for tents along creek. Across from Factory Outlet Stores, so plan to do plenty of shopping. Close to Park City attractions.

LAGOON'S PIONEER VILLAGE RV PARK & CAMPGROUND

375 N. Lagoon Drive
Salt Lake City
801-451-8100

Shady campground and full RV hookups. Next door to Lagoon Amusement Park and convenience store. Only 17 miles from downtown Salt Lake City. Open spring through fall, weather permitting.

OQUIRRH MOTOR INN

8740 North Highway 36
Lake Point 84074
801-250-0118

Camp at the foot of the Oquirrh Mountains near the shore of the Great Salt Lake. Convenient sites for RVs and lodging. Only minutes from downtown. Take I-80 W. and exit #99 at Lake Point.

SALT LAKE CITY KOA/VIP

1400 West North Temple
Salt Lake City 84116
801-328-0224 www.campvip.com

Only 1.5 miles from Temple Square. Offers cabins, as well as sites for RVs and tents. Includes a swimming pool, hot tub, and laundry facility.

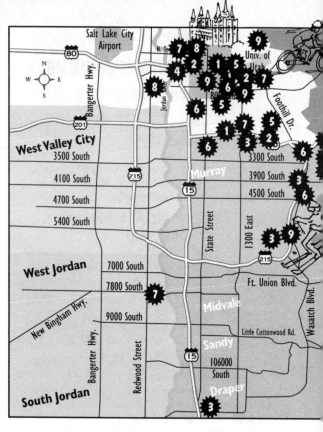

1. Antique Shops
2. Books & CD Stores
3. Factory Outlet Stores
4. Gateway Project
5. Gourmet Food Markets & Delis
6. Outdoor Specialty Stores
7. Shopping Places
8. Unique Shops
9. Vintage & Resale Shops

Salt Lake City Area

Chapter 9
UNIQUE PLACES TO SHOP

ANTIQUE SHOPS

ANTHONY'S ANTIQUES & FINE ARTS

401 East 200 South, Salt Lake City 801-328-2231

Known as a customer-friendly, and quality antique store. Amazing pieces of furniture, fountains, fireplace mantels, clocks, china, chandelier, and other fine estate pieces. Browsers welcome.

Mon. - Sat. .... 10 am - 5:30 pm

BRASS KEY ANTIQUES

43 West Broadway, Salt Lake City 801-532-2872

Housed in one of the oldest buildings in Salt Lake City. Dining room sets, bookcases, roll-top desks.

Mon. - Sat. .... 11 am - 6 pm

COBWEBS

1054 East 2100 South, Salt Lake City 801-485-9295

Located in Sugar House, loaded to the brim with antique toys, including collectibles from the 70s and 80s—like Star War action figures. Go here!

Mon. - Fri. .... 11 am - 5 pm
Saturday .... Noon - 5 pm

MORIARTY'S ANTIQUES

959 South West Temple, Salt Lake City 801-521-7207

You're at Salt Lake City's largest antique mall where you can ramble through the aisles of treasures from the 50s though the 80s.

Mon. - Sat. .... 10 am - 6 pm
Sunday .... Noon - 5 pm

SALT LAKE ANTIQUES

279 East 300 South, Salt Lake City 801-322-1273

Wall-to-ceiling merchandise that drives shoppers crazy. If you're looking for something, it's there-just find it! Antique window panes.

Mon. - Sat. .... 10 am - 6 pm

BOOKS & CD STORES

DESERET BOOKS

36 South State Street
Salt Lake City 801-328-8191

The finest bookstore in Salt Lake City, LDS Church-owned with publications intended for their members. But not any more: Books on genealogy and other sought-after resources make it a hot spot. Over 30 locations in multiple states. Own publishing division.

GRAYWHALE CD EXCHANGE

201 South 1300 East
Salt Lake City 801-583-3333

Where to find used CDs by the thousands.

Mon. - Sat. . . . . 9:30 am - 11 pm

SALT LAKE CDS

878 East 900 South
Salt Lake City 801-596-9300

Considered to have the best selection of CDs in the state, including rock, pop, and avant-garde, selling both new and used.

Mon. - Sat. . . . . 11 am - 8 pm
Sunday . . . . Noon - 5 pm

SAM WELLER BOOKS

254 South Main Street
Salt Lake City 801-328-2586

A favorite haunt for booklovers who love to browse through the store's 3 floors of books, including hard-to-find and out-of-print books. A Salt Lake institution to say the least.

FACTORY OUTLET STORES

FACTORY OUTLET STORES OF AMERICA

12101 South Factory Outlet Drive
Draper 84020, 801-571-2933

South of Salt Lake City, a 30-store outlet sells brand name merchandise for 30-70% off retail prices.

Mon. - Sat. ....10 am - 9 pm
Saturday ....Noon - 5 pm

FACTORY STORES AT PARK CITY

6699 Landmark Drive,
Park City 84098 435-645-7078

Where outlet shoppers flock by the thousands because name-brand merchants sell their products for 30-70% off retail prices. Fifty shops and restaurants.

Mon. - Sat. ....10 am - 9 pm
Sunday ....11 am - 6 pm

NORDSTROM'S RACK

2236 South 1300 East, Salt Lake City 801-484-8880

A handy outlet store for Nordstom's merchandise if you don't like paying full price at their department store.

Mon. - Sat. ....10 an - 9 pm
Sunday ....Noon - 6 pm

PATAGONICA OUTLET

3267 South Highland Drive, Holladay 801-466-2226

An outlet for the popular maker of sporting, clothes, fleece outerwear, ski underwear, and more. Slightly flawed or discontinued items.

Mon. - Sat. ....10 am - 6 pm
Sunday ....11 am - 5 pm

GATEWAY PROJECT

90 South 400 West
Salt Lake City 84101
801-366-2160

Built in time of the 2002 Olympic Games

Everything's here including the kitchen sink, when it comes to shopping. Stores for everyone's fancy, including an electronic boutique-in the newly renovated Union Pacific Railway Depot. See the new Olympic Plaza. Clothing stores, a bookstore, a sporting goods store, art galleries, and so much more.

On the entertainment side of this complex, you'll find a Build-A-Bear Workshop where you can make a teddy bear just the way you like it and take it home with you.

There are also a 12-screen movie theater with all the latest technology in surround sound and restaurants with cuisine from steaks to sushi.

For a quick bite, the food court abounds in fast food from fresh lemonade, oriental foods, pizza, to McDonalds.

Hours

Mon. - Sat. . . . . 10 am - 9 pm
Sunday . . . . Noon - 6 pm

Directions

At the old Union Pacific Railway Depot.

GOURMET MARKETS, & DELIS,

DOWNTOWN FARMER'S MARKET

Pioneer Park
300 South 300 West
Salt Lake City 801-359-5118

Summer months only. Fresh regionally grown fruits and vegetables, handicrafts, honey, jam, cheeses, salsa, and other goodies by 60 vendors who promote organic gardening. Mid-July through October.

Saturdays only .... 8 am - 1 pm

FRANK GRANOTO IMPORT CO

1391 South 300 West
Salt Lake City 801-486-5643

Italian. Imported breads, dried pasta, olive oils, sausages, cheeses, salamis, and more line the shelves. Wonderful sandwiches to die for at the counter. Frozen dishes. Stop here on your way to a picnic or outing.

Mon. - Fri. .... 8 am - 5:30 pm
Saturday .... 8 am - 5 pm

GREAT HARVEST BREAD COMPANY

905 East 900 South
Salt Lake City 801-328-2323

Favorite of locals who love their freshly baked varieties of bread and pastries. Hot bread sampling while you're buying.

Mon. - Fri. .... 6 am - 6:30 pm
Saturday .... 6 am - 6 pm

INDIA UNLIMITED

1615 South Foothill Drive, Salt Lake City 801-583-3300

Ethnic food store that offers full cooked, to-go entrees as well as ingredients to make your own.

Mon. - Thurs. .... 11 am- 8 pm
Fri. & Sat. .... 11 am - 8:30 pm

LIBERTY HEIGHTS FRESH
1242 South 1100 East
Salt Lake City 801-5FRESH
One of the best places in the city for fresh produce no matter the season, inside what was once an old gas station. Summertime, the flowers and fruits overflow the store with garage doors open.

Mon. - Sat. .... 8 am - 8:30 pm
Sunday .... 9 am - 7 pm

PIRATE O'S
11901 South 700 East
Salt Lake City 801-572-0956
A warehouse with aisles of gourmet foods at discount prices. Lots of specials too. Where to buy fancy pastas, olive oils, sausages, cheese, and more.

Mon. - Sat. .... Noon - 8 pm
Sunday .... Noon - 6 pm

TONY CAPUTO'S MARKET & DELI
308 West 300 South
Salt Lake City
Another hotspot for Italian sandwiches, salads, and desserts—eat in or take out. Deli case stocked with fine cheese, sausages, meats. Shelves loaded with sauces, pastas, and olive oils.

Daily .... 9 am - 5 pm

OUTDOOR SPECIALTY STORES

BLACK DIAMOND EQUIPMENT LIMITED

2092 East 3900 South
Salt Lake City 801-278-0233

Carries hi-tech rock climbing, mountain climbing, and backpacking gear. Caters to backcountry skiers.

DALEBOOTS

2150 South 300 West
Salt Lake City 801-487-3649

A quality custom ski-boot maker for any foot size. These won't hurt your feet–they're so comfortable.

EVOLUTION SKI COMPANY

790 West 1700 South
Salt Lake City 801-972-1144

Buy your custom-made pair of skis from this local well-known ski manufacturer. Ski repairs. Sells quality ski wear. The official 2002 Olympic ski supplier.

GUTHRIE BICYCLE

156 East 200 South
Salt Lake City 801-363-3727
www.redrocks.com

Rents bicycles to those interested in tackling the great mountain biking trails in the area. Sells top-quality bicycles and supplies.

KIRKHAM'S OUTDOOR STORE

3125 South State Street, Salt Lake City 801-486-4161

When it comes to outdoor equipment, you'll find it here. A wide selection of equipment for camping, hiking, and mountain biking. Outdoor clothing.

SALTY PEAKS SNOWBOARD SHOP

3055 East 3300 South, Salt Lake City 801-467-8000

Experienced snowboarders see the latest in snowboards and will gear you up for the slopes.

SHOPPING PLACES

CROSSROADS PLAZA

50 South Main Street
Salt Lake City 84144
801-531-1799

In the heart of downtown's attractions, Crossroads Plaza dwarfs next-door ZCMI Center Mall with 140 stores. No longer the largest indoor mall, but it use to be. Then hop next door to the ZCMI Center Mall— you haven't had enough.

Mon. - Fri. .... 10 am - 9 pm
Saturday .... Noon - 5 pm

GARDNER VILLAGE

1100 West 7800 South, West Jordan 84088
801-566-8903 www.gardner village.com

An old flour mill is now a shopper's haven. Lots of little specialty shops cluster together in a pioneer atmosphere with red brick walkways. Quilts, handicrafts, and one-of-a-kind gift shops make the way for any ladies' day out. Archibald's Restaurant bears the original pioneer miller's name, Archibald Gardner; serves lunch and dinner in what was the old mill. American dishes. The site is listed on the National Register of Historic Places. Museum on site.

(Jan. - Mar. closes at 6 pm)
Mon. - Sat. .... 10 am - 8 pm

PARK CITY MAIN STREET

Park City

Park City—a one time booming mining town—now booms with unique shops that attract shoppers by the thousands. If you love shopping, stroll along Main Street in this mountain village where every shop its own adventure. Great restaurants and art galleries.

Unique Places to Shop

SOUTH TOWNE CENTER

10450 South State Street, Sandy 801-572-1516

www.southtowncenter.com

Utah's biggest shopping mall has all the favorites like Dillard's, JC Penney, Mervyn's—150 stores in all. People say it can't be done in a day, so plan to spend lots of time shopping here.

Mon. - Sat. . . . . 10 am - 9 pm

Sunday . . . . Noon - 6 pm

SUGAR HOUSE SHOPPING DISTRICT

2100 South 700 East

Salt Lake City 801-521-9877

Eclectic shops line the street looking for shoppers.

TROLLEY SQUARE

600 South 700 East

Salt Lake City 801-521-9877

One of Salt Lake City's biggest tourist attractions—and has been since its opening in the 70s. People flock here to shop the variety of stores, restaurants, and soak up the fun atmosphere. Home of the Hard Rock Cafe, the Spaghetti Factory, and a movie theater.

Mon. - Sat. . . . . 10 am - 9 pm

Sunday . . . . Noon - 5 pm

ZCMI CENTER MALL

36 South State Street

Salt Lake City 84111

801-321-8745

The mall's location, across the street from Temple Square makes it a vital tourist attraction. More than 50 stores, including the popular ZCMI department store and Deseret Bookstore. The food court's wide variety of eateries gives sightseers a handy place to lunch before they're off to see more. Closed Sunday.

Mon. - Fri. . . . . 10 am - 9 pm

Saturday . . . . 10 am - 7 pm

UNIQUE SHOPS

ARTWORKS PARK CITY

461 Main Street
Park City 84060
435-649-4462

Art work in all types of media, whatever the artist decides to use. Selling unique pottery, glassware, jewelry, wire-wall hangings, photography, and more. Local and national artists' work.

MORMON HANDICRAFT

15 West South Temple
Salt Lake City 84101
801-355-2141

Somewhat akin to the Amish tradition of selling quilts and other fine handicrafts to tourist. A Salt Lake City destination in and of itself, taking visitors back to pioneer days—when things were much simpler? Load up before you go home, and don't forget some of the tasty fudge, made daily, for the immediate future. Ask about their recipe of the week club and you can make your fudge.

ROCKPICK LEGEND CO.

1955 North Redwood Road
Salt Lake City 84116
801-355-7952

Shop where it really rocks. Discover this rock shop's legendary supply of rocks, fossils, rare gems, minerals, and other rock-related goodies. Big rock yard—any rockhound's dream.

Mon. - Sat. . . . . 9:30 am - 6 pm
Sunday . . . . 9 am - 3 pm

VINTAGE & RESALE SHOPS

DESERET INDUSTRIES
743 West 700 South
Salt Lake City 801-579-1200

A giant LDS-owned thrift store where one man's junk is another's treasure, and the price is always right. Established in 1938 to help the needy. No frills shopping, but endless possibilities. Forty-six other locations, including the Western states.

Mon. - Sat. .... 10 am - 6 pm

GARP'S MERCANTILE
627 South State Street
Salt Lake City 801-537-1357

Specializing in vintage and antique clothing but now carries unusual comtemporary items too.

GRUNTS & POSTURES
779 East 300 South
Salt Lake City 801-521-3202

Not too far from the university's student body, who loves to haunt this place. Selling vintage clothing that puts adds funkiness to anyone's wardrobe, including your Halloween costume.

PIB'S EXCHANGE
2144 South Highland Drive
Salt Lake City 801-484-7996

Picky about what they sell so you can be too. Quality name-brand clothing for a fraction of the price—used. Bargains on snowboarding clothes, ski outfits, shoes, shorts, shirts, and all types of casual clothing. Diesel jeans for $30. Vintage clothing too.

Mon. - Fri. .... 11 am - 9 pm
Saturday .... 11 am -8 pm
Sunday .... 1 pm - 5 pm

Chapter 10
WATCH FOR THESE ANNUAL EVENTS

DAYS OF `47
801-254-2524
July
Utah celebrates its heritage

Brigham Young led the Mormon pioneers into the Salt Lake Valley through Emigration Canyon on July 24, 1847. The Days of '47 celebration honors those early settlers and is one of Utah's biggest events.

The month of July is filled with activities that lead up to the big day, July 24th. On that day, the Days of '47 Parade is one of the oldest and largest parades in the United States. Colorful floats, marching bands, clowns, and horses fill the streets. Over a hundred entries in the parade. Bleacher seats available through the Daughters of the Utah Pioneer Museum, 801-538-1050. Admission charged.

Other events include the Days of '47 World Championship Rodeo at the Delta Center, the All-Horse Parade (over 1200 horses), the Youth Parade, fireworks, and other shows.

Hours
Parade
July 24th . . . . 9 am

Cost
Free

Directions
Parade route: Starts at South Temple and Main Streets. Then East to 200 East, south to 900 South, and east to Liberty Park (600 East).

GREEK FESTIVAL

279 South 300 West
Salt Lake City 84101
801-328-9681

September

Any worthwhile ethnic festival has to do with food, and this festival does its job. Save room for the tasty desserts. And the cooking demonstrations send you home to cook your own. The festival kicks off Saturday's festivities with a 5K run and a 1-mile walk. Friday is the Opening Ceremony. Work up an appetite for feasting on great Greek food.

A 3-day festival—the largest ethnic festival in Utah. Held annually at the Holy Trinity Cathedral. Here's your chance to tour the church and see the Hellenic Cultural Museum in the basement. Greek music, dancing, and booths.

Hours

The 1st weekend after Labor Day.

Cost

Adults $2
Children $1

Directions

At the Holy Trinity Cathedral.

LIVING TRADITIONS FESTIVAL

451 South State Street
Salt Lake City 84102
801-533-5760

May

It's like a trip around the world without paying airfare. A 3-day weekend when Utah celebrates its broad ethnic heritage. Feast on exotic delicacies from countries like Thailand, Spain, El Salvador, Mexico, Germany, and Lebanon. Cultural activities and booths. Educational as well as fun. Bring the whole family.

Held annually at Washington Square at the City and County Building grounds.

Cost

Free

Directions

On Washington Square.

SUNDANCE FILM FESTIVAL

328 Main Street
Park City 84060
801-328-3456

January

Mingle with celebrities at this 10-day independent film festival held at different places in Park City and in Salt Lake City.

Founded by Robert Redford, the festival is dedicated to artists of independent and documentary films and the exhibition of their works. Thousands of such films are submitted every year, hoping to win.

Tickets go on sale a few days before the event and sell out quickly.

Cost

$6 - $16

Directions

In Park City and different venues
in Salt Lake City.

TWILIGHT CONCERT SERIES

36 East 200 South
Salt Lake City
801-359-5118

Mid-July to Mid-August

Enjoy a spectacular concert series that takes place on Thursday nights from mid-July though mid-August. Outstanding performances by top musicians make it an event you don't want to miss. Concerts start right after sunset at 8 pm.

Good food goes well with good music. About 5 pm the food and craft booths open with food from local restaurants and crafts from local artisans. Many bring their own picnic and a blanket.

What an ideal way to spend a summer's evening.

Hours

Food Market . . . . 5 pm
Thursdays . . . . 8 pm

Cost
Free

Directions
Gallivan Center, downtown.

UTAH ARTS FESTIVAL

331 W. Pierpont
Salt Lake City 84101
801-322-2428

June

Once a year for 4 days, Salt Lake City celebrates the arts with a festival that draws over 80,000 art-lovers. Visit the Artists' Marketplace with works for sale by local and well-known professional artists in all types of media. Watch street theater, or live musical entertainment. And that's not all—the festival takes in the literary arts too.

Cost

Adults	$7.50
Seniors	$3
Children under age 12	Free

Directions

At Main St. and 3rd South.

UTAH SHAKESPEAREAN FESTIVAL

351 West Center Street, Cedar City 84720
435-586-7878 800-752-9849
www.bard.org

May - October

Not much to do in small town Cedar City after the sun goes down? No problem. Over 150,000 people come here each year to see one of the finest Shakespearean festivals in the country. This town's Tony Award-winning theater offers six productions annually in an authentic Shakespearean theater.

But that's not all. Take a tour of their backstage, or show up early in the evening for the Greenshow—boisterous singing, dancing, magic, and juggling acts. Enjoy the evening's Royal Feaste: a five-course meal served as it would have been in Shakespeare's time. By reservation only before noon on date of performance. Plan to purchase your tickets in advance; many performances sell out. Matinee shows too.

Hours
Summer Performances
Mon. - Sat. . . . . 8 pm
Greenshow . . . . 7 pm
Royal Feaste
Tues., Wed., Fri., & Sat., ... 5:30 pm
Cost
Evening performances . . . . Prices vary
Backstage tour $7
Royal Feaste $30
Directions
From I-15 S., exit Cedar City exit #62.

163

Chapter 11
WHAT TO DO IN PARK CITY?

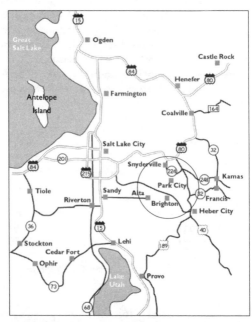

ARTS & MUSEUMS

EGYPTIAN THEATRE

328 Main Street, 435-649-9371

Patterned after the Egyptian Theater in Pasadena, California. Built in the early 1900s, now a Park City landmark and home of the Egyptian Theatre Company. Offers avant-garde to musicals. Tickets at box office.

PARK CITY HISTORICAL SOC. & MUSEUM

528 Main Street, 435-649-6104

A museum that explains the history of this one-time mining country, now a world-class ski resort. Located in the old 1884 City Hall building. See a restored stagecoach. Learn about the Great Fire of 1898 that destroyed Main Street. To help, the railroad donated materials to rebuild.

Mon. - Sat. .... 10 am - 7 pm
Sunday .... Noon - 6 pm

PARK CITY FILM SERIES

1255 Park Avenue 435-615-8291 parkcityfilmseries.com

Watch the Sundance Film Festival's favorites and other independent films at the Jim Santy Auditorium, Fri. & Sat. at 8 pm.

SUMMIT COUNTY COURTHOUSE MUSEUM

60 N. Main Street, Coalville
435-336-3015 www.co.summit.ut.us

Learn the area's history of coal mining at this fascinating museum housed in the old 1904 Summit County Courthouse. Find exhibits on the lumber industry, a juke box, and more.

Mon. - Fri. .... 8 am - 5 pm

NATIONAL ABILITY CENTER

3351 West Highway 248
Park City 84098
435-649-3991
www.nationalabilitycenter.org

Special facility for those with special abilities

Since 1985, a center with year-round and seasonal activities for people with disabilities: skiing, snowboarding, swimming, cycling, waterskiing, horseback riding, rafting, camping trips, indoor rockclimbing, scuba diving, and more. All ages can participate and activities can include families, friends, and groups. Activities are geared for those with orthopedic, spinal cord, neuromuscular, visual, and hearing impairments, cognitive and developmental disabilities. Winter ski programs at Park City Mountain Resort.

Hours

Mon. - Sat. . . . . 8:30 am - 5 pm

Cost

Varies with activities

Directions

Hwy 40 and Hwy 248. From Hwy 40, exit #4.

NATIONAL SPORTS FOUNDATIONS

P.O. Box 682722
Park City 84068
435-645-7660

Professional youth programs for ski jumping

Learn ski jumping and Nordic combination—ski jumping and cross-country skiing sports—using the Utah Olympic Park's outstanding facilities. Sign up for sessions with a qualified instructor. Geared for children ages 8 to 18. Offers a summer session, a winter session, and after-school programs.

Directions

Located at the Jump Center at the base of the jumping hills in Utah Olympic Park.

OUTDOOR RECREATION

ALPINE SLIDE

1310 Lowell Avenue, Park City 435-649-8111
Take the chair lift to the top of the mountain at
Park City Mountain Ski Resort, then slide back down
on a sled. You travel up to 25 mph, but you control
how fast you go. Open the end of May to October.

GORGOZA PARK TUBING

435-658-2648 www.parkcitymountain.com
A snow tubing playground. Offers lift-serviced tube
rides, mini snowmobiles for kids, and a lift-services
jib park, where skiers and riders can practice.

HOMESTEAD RESORT SCUBA DIVING

800-327-7220 435-654-1102
www.homesteadresort.com
Year-round scuba diving in warm-water crater lake.
Snorkeling, swimming, and theapeutic mineral bathing.

NORWEGIAN OUTDOOR EXPLORATION

800-649-5322 435-649-5322
www.outdoorcenter.org
Your choice of snowshoes or cross-country skis
for private guided tours into the backcountry.

PARK CITY SNOWSHOE ADVENTURES

435-640-2573 801-209-4479
www.parkcitysnowshoe.com
Snowshoe into the backcountry with a gourmet
meal and guide. Your trip ends with a massage.

WASATCH POWDERBIRD GUIDE

877-974-4354 435-649-9422
Offers helicopter skiing in the Wasatch Mountains.
Helicopter shuttles from Deer Valley to Snowbird
Resorts. Scenic rides.

PARK CITY SKI RESORTS

THE CANYONS SKI RESORT

4000 The Canyon Resort Drive
Park City
435-6449-5400
www.thecanyons.com

Utah's newest ski resort–the 5th largest in the U.S. Ski over 8 mountains on 16 chair lifts. Take scenic rides on the gondola during the summer. Great hiking and mountain biking trails.

Daily . . . . 9 am - 4 pm

DEER PARK SKI RESORT

2250 Deer Valley Drive
Park City 84060
435-649-1000

Chosen for the 2002 Olympic freestyle mogul and aerial events. Boasts of having a 120-day ski season. Ski 4 mountains on 19 chair lifts, over 88 runs. Considered one of the 10 best places to mountain bike.

Daily . . . . 9 am - 4:15 pm

PARK CITY MOUNTAIN RESORT

1310 Lowell Avenue
Park City
435-649-8111

Utah's premier ski resort. Host of the 2002 Olympic Winter Games alpine giant slalom and snowboarding events. Also hosts the alpine World Cup circuit every November. Offers 3300 acres of skiable terrain with 14 chairlifts including 4 high-speed chairs. Also has ability to cover 475 acres with man-made snow. Known for its wonderfully groomed slopes. Prime mountain biking trails. Ski and snowboarding schools.

Daily . . . . 9 am - 4 pm

SKI EQUIPMENT RENTALS

ALOHA SKI & SNOWBOARD
Park City Mountain Resort, Park City 435-649-9690
Ski & snowboard rentals, tune-ups, storage, retail.
Clothing rentals. Snowshoe rentals.

DESTINATION SPORTS
Town Lift, Park City Mountain Resort, The Canyons
Park City 435-649-4806
Ski & snowboard rentals, tune-ups, storage, retail.
Clothing rentals. Snowshoe rentals.

GART SPORTS
1780 Park Avenue, Park City
435-649-6922
Ski, snowshoe & snowboard rentals, tune-ups,
storage, retail. X-C rentals.

JAKE'S SKI RENTALS
Park City Mountain Resort, Park City
435-645-9736
Ski, clothing, snowboard rentals, tune-ups, retail.

JAN'S MOUNTAIN OUTFITTERS
1600 Park Avenue, Park City Mountain Resort, Deer
Valley Resort 435-649-4949
Ski & snowboard rentals, tune-ups, retail.

KINDERSPORT JUNIOR SKI & OUTFITTERS
Park City Mountain Resort, Park City
435-649-5463
Ski rentals and retail.

MAX SNOWBOARD RENTALS
Park City Mountain Resort & The Canyons
Park City 435-647-9699
Snowboard rentals, clothing, storage, retail.

UTAH OLYMPIC PARK
3000 Bear Hollow Drive
Park City 84060
435-658-4200
www.saltlake2002.com

Pretend you're an Olympian for a day

Built for the 2002 Olympic Winter Games. The world's highest ski jumping hills, at an elevation of 7116 feet above sea level. Offers year-round training for athletes with nerves of steel from around the world. Watch them in action any day but Monday.

Tour the park on a shuttle. It takes an hour, giving insights into sports at hand: bobsled, luge, skeleton, as well as Nordic ski jumping. Watch the videos.

During the summer, watch freestyle aerialists jump, landing into the 750,000-gallon training pool. You also can experience the thrill of jumping into training pools from the smaller hills.

In the winter, try ski jumping on the smaller hills, ride down the bobsled, luge, and skeleton track with a professional driver and brakeman.

The 389-acre park includes a day lodge with a sport shop and a deli.

Hours
Tours
Daily .... 11 am, 12:30 pm & 2 pm

Cost
Entrance fee
Per Car $5
Shuttle tour $3

Directions
Located 25 minutes from downtown.
Take I-80 E. to Park City.

WHERE TO EAT?

350 MAIN NEW AMERICAN BRASSERIE

350 Main Street, Park City 435-649-3140

$$$ Inside one of Main Street's historic buildings. Upscale food and service. American. dinner only.

EATING ESTABLISHMENT

317 Main Street, Park City 435-649-8284

$$ A favorite for hot home-style soups, salads, and sandwiches. Best hamburgers in town. Great breakfasts.

GRAPPO ITALIAN RESTAURANT

151 Main Street, Park City 435-645-0636

$$$ Open for dinner. Elegant restaurant serving regional Italian cuisine.

MAIN STREET PIZZA & NOODLE

530 Main Street Park City 435-645-8878

$$ Tasty California-style pizza from scratch. Pasta dishes, salads, and sandwiches. Family-friendly.

SAGE GRILL

6300 N. Sagewood Drive, Park City 435-658-2267

$$$ Signature dishes created from California cuisine. Casual, delightful atmosphere. Kids menu.

SNAKE CREEK GRILL

650 West 100 South, Heber City 435-654-2133

$$$$ High popularity in a rustic setting. Chef offers nightly specials. Reservations recommended. Outdoor dining with a mountain view. Wed. - Sun.

TEXAS RED'S PIT BARBECUE

440 Main Street, Park City 435-649-REDS

$$ Open daily with ribs, pork shoulder, brisket, chicken, turkey, sausage, and more from their huge wood-fired pits. Kids menu.

WHERE TO STAY?

BEST WESTERN LANDMARK INN

6560 N. Landmark Dr. 435-649-7300 bwlandmarkinn.com
AAA, 3-Diamond hotel. Deluxe continental breakfast. Free ski shuttle. Indoor pool, spa. $79-$300.

GRAND SUMMIT HOTEL

4000 Canyons Resort Dr. 435-615-8040 thecanyons.com
Luxury hotel at the Canyons Resort. Child care. Health club. Ski from lodge. I-80 E. to Kimball Junction; south on SR-224. Right on Parkwest Dr. $129-$1589.

HOLIDAY INN EXPRESS HOTEL

1501 W. Ute Boulevard 435-658-1600 utahhospitality.com
Offers 2-person Jacuzzi and steamer suites. Free transportation to ski resorts and Main Street. Free Breakfast. Indoor pool, fitness center. $99-$279.

OLD MINER'S LODGE

615 Woodside 435-645-8068 www.oldminerslodge.com
Bed & Breakfast. Named one of America's top inns and one of Park City's oldest. Next to chair lift. Full breakfast included. $105-$270.

PARK CITY MARRIOTT

1895 Sidewinder Drive 435-649-2900 parkcityutah.com
New. Deluxe rooms and suites. Full service. Restaurant. Hot tub, indoor pool. $199-$269.

SILVER KING HOTEL

1485 Empire Avenue 435-649-3700 silverkinghotel.com
Luxurious AAA, 4-Diamond condominium hotel next to Park City Mt. Resort. Fireplace, jetted tubs, Fully equipped kitchens.$175-$765.

STEIN ERIKSEN LODGE

7700 Stein Way 435-649-3700 steinlodge.com
Elegant Norwegian lodge, fine dining. $575-$1475.

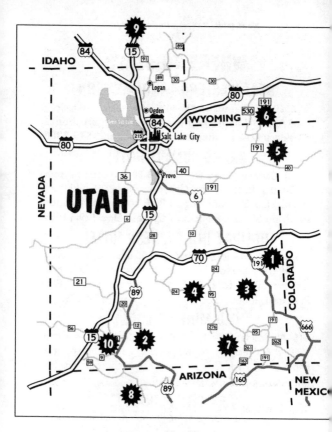

1. Arches National Park
2. Bryce Canyon National Park
3. Canyonlands National Park
4. Capitol Reef National Park
5. Dinosaur National Monument
6. Flaming Gorge National Recreation Area
7. Glen Canyon National Recreation Area
8. Grand Canyon National Park (North Rim)
9. Yellowstone National Park
10. Zion National Park

Chapter 12
SCENIC
NATIONAL PARKS

ARCHES NATIONAL PARK

P.O. Box 907
Moab 84532
435-719-2299
www.nps.gov/arch

Desert sandstone arches everywhere

See the world's largest concentration of stone arches—over 2000. Drive the park's 40-mile paved road past famous geological features: Fiery Furnace, Balanced Rock, Skyline Arch, Double Arch, and more. Best of all, view them from your car.

Popular activities include hiking, backpacking, and rock climbing; permits required. Biking allowed on roads only. Hike the popular Delicate Arch trail; it's 3 miles round trip. Guided walks with a ranger offered in the summer; sign up at the visitor center. Summer temperatures can reach 100 degrees Fahrenheit. Bring along plenty of water.

Hours

(Closed Christmas Day)
Visitor Center
Daily (Apr. - Sept.) . . . . . . 7:30 am - 6 pm
Daily (Winter) . . . . 8 am - 4:30 pm
Park
24 Hours/7days

Cost

Entrance Fee
Per Vehicle $10
Per Person $5

Directions

230 Miles from Salt Lake City
From US 191, enter the park 5 miles
north of Moab.

BRYCE CANYON NATIONAL PARK

P.O. Box 170001, Bryce Canyon 84717
435-834-5322 www.nps.gov/brca

Rock spires jut out of the earth in huge maze

It took millions of years to create the thousands of delicately carved, brilliantly colored spires and pinnacles at Bryce Canyon. Drive the 37-mile loop or take the convenient shuttle past the park's famous view points like Sunrise, Sunset, Rainbow, and Inspiration Points. Don't miss Fairyland. Brilliant hues at sunrise or sunset. Shuttle available May - October only. Hiking is popular along the rim and canyon bottom. Ask about the park's special activities like the moon walks and star talks at the visitor center. A favorite place for cross-country skiers and snowshoers. Requires 18 inches of snow. Check out snowshoes free of charge, including children's sizes, at the visitor center. Horseback riding available. Biking allowed only on paved roads. The Bryce Lodge is a National Historic Landmark, open April - November. Visitor center and park open year-round. Camping.

Hours
Visitor Center
(Closed Thanksgiving, Christmas, New Year's Day)

Daily (summer) . . . . 8 am - 8 pm
Park 24 Hours/7Days

Cost: Entrance Fee

Per Vehicle (7 day pass) $20
Shuttle ride (7 day pass) . . . . $15/per car

Directions

260 miles from Salt Lake City

Take I-15 S. to exit #95 (Hwy 20) to Hwy 89 S. On Hwy 89, turn east on Hwy 12 (7 miles south of Panguith) and go to junction Hwy 12 & Hwy 63. Turn south onto Hwy 63 for 3 miles to park's entrance.

CANYONLANDS NATIONAL PARK

2282 South West Resource Boulevard, Moab 84532
435-719-2313 www.nps.gov/cany

Utah's largest national park awaits you

It's not possible to see this park in a day. Plan to see 1 or 2 districts in a single trip; travel between districts requires 2 to 6 hours by car. World-renowned 4-wheel driving, mountain biking, backpacking, and whitewater rafting. Permits required. Camping allowed, but no fires, no pets. Bring drinking water.

The Colorado and Green Rivers sliced the area into 4 parts. The Island in the Sky district is most accessible and the easiest to visit in a short period of time. All other destinations require some boating, hiking, or 4-wheel driving to see attractions. The Needles district offers scenic arches, rock spires, deep canyons, potholes, and prehistoric ruins. The Maze district is most remote and includes maze-like canyons and huge colorful free-standing rocks. The rivers make up the 4th district.

Hours: Visitor Centers
(Closed Christmas Day & New Year's Day)
Daily .... 8 am - 4:30 pm
Park
24 Hours/7 Days
Cost: Entrance Fee
Per vehicle $10
Per person $5
Directions
349 Miles from Salt Lake City
Two paved entrances into Canyonlands: Hwy 313 leads to the Island in the Sky District and is 10 miles north of Moab; Hwy 211 leads to the Needles District and is 40 miles south of Moab. Roads to the Maze District are a mixture of graded dirt and only for 4WD. These roads may become impassable when wet.

CAPITOL REEF NATIONAL PARK

HC 70 Box 15
Torrey 84775
435-425-3791
www.nps.gov/care

Hit this park's scenic road for some fun

Utah Highway 24 runs east and west through this park. Drive the 25-mile scenic round trip that begins at the visitor center. Other interesting dirt roads traverse the park from the main road. Check weather conditions before heading out.

Brilliant colored sandstone formations and cliffs. Bright red rocks and ancient petroglyphs. See Waterpocket Fold—a 100-mile long wrinkle in the earth's crust protected by the park.

Large orchards planted by early settlers offer fresh fruit for picking in the summer.

Park and campgrounds are open year-round.

Hours

Visitor Center
(Closed Christmas Eve and Day)
Daily (Summer) .... 8 am - 6 pm
Daily .... 8 am - 4:30 pm
Park
24 Hours/7 Days

Cost

Entrance Fee
Per vehicle for scenic drive $5

Directions

229 Miles from Salt Lake City
Located in south-central Utah on Utah Hwy 24.

DINOSAUR NATIONAL MONUMENT

Quarry Visitor Center
Box 128, Jensen, Utah 84035   435-789-2115
www.nps.gov/dino

They've got a bone to pick

In 1909, paleontologist Earl Douglas discovered a huge sandbar layered with prehistoric plants and animals fossils. In 1915, the quarry became a national monument; later a visitor center was built over the top of it for protection. See over 2000 dinosaur bones in the sandstone wall. Watch paleontologists at work: chipping away at the sandstone, exposing the fossils. Look inside the laboratory where the fossilized bones are preserved.

The park stretches east into Colorado. Famous for Indian rock art. Hiking trails and camping available. Popular for whitewater rafting on the Green and Yampa Rivers past towering red cliffs, wildlife, and Indian ruins. Floaters must obtain permits from rangers.

Hours
Open year-round

Daily (summer) . . . . 8 am - 6 pm
Weekdays (winter) . . . . . . 8 am - 4:30 pm

Cost
Entrance Fee

Winter months . . . . Free
Per vehicle (7-day pass) $10
Individual (7-day pass) $5

Directions
185 Miles from Salt Lake City

For the Utah visitor center, take Hwy 40 to Jensen, (southeast of Vernal), then Hwy 149 north 7 miles to the park's entrance.

FLAMING GORGE NATIONAL RECREATION AREA

P.O. Box 279, Manila 84046
435-784-3445
435-885-3305 Flaming Gorge Dam Visitor Center

A boater's paradise

John Wesley Powell and his 9 men explored the Green River in small wooden boats in the spring of 1869. He named the canyon Flaming Gorge when they saw the impressive sight of the sun's reflection the red rocks. Today, the recreational area encompassas 207,363 acres of land and water. Half of the area lies in Utah, the other half in Wyoming.

Scenic Flamimg Gorge Reservoir was formed by the Green River–a haven for all kinds of water sports. It's also popular for trophy-size trout. The reservoir's high elevation of 6040 feet keeps its summer temperature a constant 80 degrees.

See twisted rock formations located west of Flaming Gorge in Sheep Creek Canyon Geological Area.

Visitors can take a self-guided tour of the dam that descends 500 feet inside the huge concrete structure, offered seasonally. Visitor centers at the Flaming Gorge Dam, open year-round, and at Red Canyon Overlook, open seasonally. Plenty of camping and hiking trails.

Hours
Open year-round
Cost
Entrance Fee
Day use pass $2
Directions
160 Miles from Salt Lake City
Take U.S. 40 E. to Vernal, Utah., then
U.S. 191 north.

GLEN CANYON NATIONAL RECREATION AREA

Bullfrog Visitor Center
435-684-7400
www.nps.gov/glca

Explore to your heart's content

Lake Powell is the 2nd largest reservoir in North America, 186 miles long. Has 1960 acres of shoreline. Visit Rainbow Bridge—considered one of 7 natural wonders of the world. Half-day and full-day tours offered. Numerous side canyons and inlets make this lake a boater's paradise. Many of the coves are hiding places for old Indian ruins. Popular for renting houseboats, bass fishing, water skiing, four-wheel driving, and photography.

Hours

Bullfrog Visitor Center
(April - October)

Daily . . . . 8 am - 5 pm

Cost

Entrance Fee

Per vehicle $10
Pedestrian $3

Directions

299 Miles from Salt Lake City

The Bullfrog Visitor Center is located south on Hwy 276. Halls Crossing is also reached on Hwy 276. Hite Ranger Station is located on Hwy 95.

GRAND CANYON NATIONAL PARK (NORTH RIM)

P.O. Box 129
Grand Canyon, AZ 86023
520-638-7888
www.nps.gov/grca

Look what the Colorado River did

Grand Canyon National Park lies within northern Arizona. It encompasses 277 miles of the Colorado River, over 1 million acres of land. Spectacular, considered the world's greatest example of erosion— no other place like it on earth. At the canyon's deepest point, it plunges 6000 feet below the rim.

The North Rim, a thousand feet higher in elevation than the more heavily visited South Rim, is only open mid-May through mid-October. Plans for lodging should be made well in advanced. Parking is also limited, so arrive early. Especially popular for hiking, backpacking, camping, biking, horseback riding, mule rides, and whitewater rafting. Hiking rim to rim takes about 3 days one-way. A trip to the canyon's bottom and back takes 2 days. Rafters spend up to 2 weeks floating through the canyon.

Hours

Daily (visitor center) .... 8 am - 6 pm

Cost

Per vehicle (7 day pass) $20
Per Individual (7 day pass) $10

Directions

299 Miles from Salt Lake City
Travel 44 miles south of Jacob Lake, AZ, via Hwy 67.

YELLOWSTONE NATIONAL PARK

P.O. Box 168
Yellowstone National Park, WY 82190
307-344-7381
www.nps.gov/yell

Visit the world's 1st national park

Within a day's drive of Salt Lake City lie a number of world-renowned national parks. Yellowstone Park is no exception. Almost 3 million people come every year to see this magnificent park. It has 2 million acres of scenic bliss: numerous waterfalls, steaming geysers, an abundance of wildlife, and over 1100 miles of hiking trails.

Stay overnight at Old Faithful Lodge. Built in 1904, there's nothing else like it. Has a 65-foot ceiling, a massive rhyolite fireplace, and made from lodge pole pines. It is listed as a National Historic Landmark. Make reservations well in advance.

Hours

Seasonal

Cost

Entrance Fee

Per vehicle (7-day pass) $20
Individual (7-day pass) $10

Directions

369 Miles from Salt Lake City

From Salt Lake City, take I-15 N. (212 miles) into Idaho. Exit #119 and go east (121 miles) on US 20 into Montana, then Wyoming. Travel northeast on US 89 (13.2 miles) and east on Norris Canyon Rd. (11.5 miles). Turn right onto Grand Loop Rd. (6.7 miles) and watch for signs.

ZION NATIONAL PARK

P.O. Box 1099
Springdale 84767
435-772-3256
www.nps.gov/zion/

Nature's the artist

A national park created in 1919, one of our country's oldest. Now attracts nearly 3 million people a year. You can no longer drive through the park in the summer; visitors must ride the shuttle. Most, however, find it a delightful way to see the canyon's fascinating formations.

Although there are 2 entrances to the park, the East Entrance is more dramatic. The road drops through a mile-long tunnel and has switchbacks down into the canyon.

Hiking is most popular. Some trails are even suitable for strollers and wheelchairs, others are more challenging. The visitor centers are open year-round.

Hours

Visitors Centers
(Hours vary spring and fall)

Daily (summer) .... 8 am - 8 pm
Daily (winter) .... 8 am - 4:30 pm

Cost

Entrance Fee

Per car $20
Pedestrians & bicycles $10

Directions

390 Miles from Salt Lake City

Two entrances. From I-15 travel 33 miles east on Hwy 9 for the East Entrance or from I-89 travel 12 miles west on Hwy 9 for the South Entrance.

Index

Index

Index

Index

Index